MR ATHERSTONE
LEAVES THE STAGE

THE BATTERSEA
MURDER MYSTERY

RICHARD WHITTINGTON-EGAN

First published 2015

Amberley Publishing
The Hill, Stroud
Gloucestershire, GL5 4EP

www.amberley-books.com

British Library Cataloguing in Publication Data.
A catalogue record for this book is available from the British Library.

ISBN 978 1 4456 4544 5 (paperback)
ISBN 978 1 4456 4552 0 (ebook)

Typesetting and Origination by Amberley Publishing.
Printed in Great Britain.

Contents

Contents

Part One
Battersea – The Backdrop

The land that was to become Battersea Park, the area's distinguishing feature, was originally known as Battersea Fields. It was a terrain largely occupied by asparagus growers, whose produce, when prepared for sale, was known as a Battersea Bunch.

It was Mr Thomas Cubitt, the builder, who converted the swampy marshes into a park.

The creation of Battersea's park meant that, on 22 August 1853, the Tivoli Tea Garden and Pleasure Ground, a sort of second Vauxhall Gardens, was closed. Having initially attracted a number of aristocrats to Battersea it had subsequently earned itself a bad reputation, becoming a hotbed of drinking, gambling, donkey races and fortune tellers. Possession was also obtained, and closure effected, of the Red House Tavern, which was a favoured haunt of Charles Dickens. The tavern and the tea garden had both been prime Battersea attractions.

The park opened in 1858. Improvements followed. In 1860 a large expanse of lake was added, and in May 1885 the Albert Palace, which was originally built for the Dublin International Exhibition of 1872, was re-erected on a more or less derelict site on the south side of the park. Specialising in high-class musical entertainment and possessed of a very fine picture gallery, the palace, which opened its doors in June 1885, was culturally eminently acceptable; but, despite cat, bird and flower shows, an impressive aquarium and such ventures as the importation from India of silk spinners, weavers, carpet makers, metalworkers, embroiderers, singers, dancers and snake charmers, it never proved a popular success. After remaining closed for many years, it was finally demolished about 1894. Its site was partly covered by the Battersea Polytechnic and partly by York Mansions. Sparrows nested in the demolished palace's great organ – pride of the Connaught Hall Concert Room – which, rescued, was taken to Fort Augustus Abbey in Scotland.

The entire south side of the perimeter of the park

consists of a half-mile of large blocks of residential flats, forming Prince of Wales Drive. Over the years they housed some celebrated tenants, such as Nöel Coward and Sean O'Casey. Philip Gibbs published, in 1930, a novel, *Intellectual Mansions*, which was centred upon the lives and vagaries of the inhabitants of the stretch of Prince of Wales Drive residences. Albert Bridge Road, on the west side, is likewise made up of mansion blocks of flats, as well as some good-class houses. On the east side were the tracks and yards of the Southern Railway, screened from view by an ornamental wall, which had been put up in Battersea Park Road by the former London, Brighton & South Coast Railway.

During the early days of cycling, about 1896, Battersea Park became the fashionable rendezvous for London society, who used to frequent it before breakfast, either to take a bicycle ride themselves or to see the attractive 'New Women' of the period whizzing by on two wheels. Battersea Park was also the place where cricket matches used to be played, attracting quite large numbers of spectators.

The great Battersea Fun Fair, held in the park during the Festival of Britain in 1951, was a runaway success. One of the many celebrated visitors was the film star Elizabeth Taylor.

I remember, too, the excitement of the Tree-Walk; of strolling nonchalantly through the green leaves, high above the lamplit avenue of little booths where fortune tellers, palms crossed with silver, plied their gifts, and where there were folk selling sweets, multi-coloured ice cream, peanuts and what-have-you, as well as a tempting selection of small and outlandish inedible novelty goods. Nor must one forget the beautiful underground grotto, with its intercommunicating chambers, walls covered with sparkling stones and shells; or the charming little zoo, and its good-natured occupants.

I lived for twenty years in Albert Mansions, in Albert

Bridge Road, where I had been preceded some seventy-two years earlier by Annie Dowson, the mother of the nineties poet Ernest Dowson. She lived in No. 7. After her husband's death there she found the flat overlooking Battersea Park unbearable, and moved to lodgings at Lee, in Kent, where, sad to relate, she committed suicide, hanging herself with a handkerchief tied to the rail of her bedstead. She was only forty-six years old.

It was in Albert Mansions, too, that Tessa Dahl's mother, the Broadway actress and Oscar-winning Hollywood film star Patricia Neal, lived. She was recovering from a series of three massive strokes that had left her paralysed, unable to walk, partially blind in one eye, and with seriously impaired speech. I would often see her and her divorced husband, Roald Dahl, who was a regular visitor. Happily, she made a more or less complete recovery. She returned to her native America, dying of lung cancer in August 2010, aged eighty-four.

Every so often I would desert Battersea, trudging over the narrow pavement of the Albert Bridge into Chelsea, where, at her home in Lawrence Street, Camille Wolff, under the banner of Grey House Books, ran the business of selling from a vast stock of criminous volumes. The books were stacked everywhere, including in the lavatory, where books on the Mafia were on view. Camille, who died in September 2014, aged 102, was a great character. She was born in Didsbury, south Manchester. Her father was a trader in textiles, her mother a member of the Sieff family, among the founders of Marks & Spencer. Camille grew up in Egypt, but was despatched to a boarding school in England and subsequently studied medicine at Manchester University. A fully qualified doctor, she did not practise, but, suffering from deafness, pursued a career in occupational health. After her retirement she presided over a salon which attracted crime buffs from all over the world, and she was a generous hostess, throwing splendiferous luncheon and dinner parties. I recall in particular the gathering at which humble Ripper enthusiasts rubbed shoulders with many of the big-name Ripper specialists. Camille's sole anxiety on these occasions was that the guests should be careful not to sit on Fred, one of her well-beloved cats.

On the serious side, Battersea offers its Old Church, St Mary's, where Turner used to paint sunsets, setting up his easel on the river foreshore; where William Blake was married, and where that great practitioner of venenation Dr Thomas Smethurst bigamously married his victim. And there is Battersea Old House, the brooding abode of ghosts.

Battersea offers, too, a particularly horrible crime. In the year 1873 the even tenor of Battersean life was brutally ruptured by what came to be known as the Battersea Barbarity. At about 6.30 a.m. on Friday 5 September 1873, a galley of the Thames Police was on patrol on the Thames. Having come from Somerset House, they were rowing upriver towards Chelsea Bridge. It was as they were passing close to the Battersea Waterworks that one of the three police officers aboard, Constable Richard Fane, spotted, lying on the mud of the waterworks' foreshore, what he thought to be the carcass of a dead animal. The tide was very near low water, and Fane put the galley ashore and told one of his brother officers to get out and investigate. In urgent tones the investigating officer called out to Fane to come and see. To his horror he found himself confronted by a human body – the headless, armless, legless, cut-up quarter of a woman's torso. Recovering his equipoise, Fane took the gruesome piece of flesh on board the galley and delivered it to the Thames Police Station Ship, the *Royalist*, off the Thames Embankment. He was directed, however, by his superior officer to take the torso back to the parish where he had found it. He did so, and the inspector at Battersea Police Station sent for Dr Kempster, the divisional surgeon.

The discovery of these bits and pieces of a human

body in the Thames excited a reactive horror akin to that caused by a similar discovery sixteen years before, when, in 1857, a bag of bones was found at the foot of Rennie's old Waterloo Bridge. In the early morning grey of 9 October 1857, two boys, rowing up the Thames, saw, lodged upon the abutment at the foot of one of the bridge's Doric columns, an object which upon inspection proved to be a carpet bag. Upon still closer inspection, at Bow Street Police Station, it was found to contain, not the modest treasure for which the lads had hoped, but twenty assorted pieces of a human body. The bones had been sawn through; the flesh, cleanly cut, had been boiled and pickled in brine. These sad *reliquiae* were accompanied by a selection of men's clothing – coat, waistcoat, surtout, vest, drawers, shirt, trousers and socks. The garments, carrying no labels, were of distinctly foreign cut. There was no head, but short lengths of dark hair marked the body as that of an adult.

Mr Paynter, the divisional police surgeon, who made an examination of the fragmentary remains, noted a wound between the fourth and fifth ribs on the left side, caused by a very sharp instrument, such as a stiletto. This was, in his view, the likely cause of death. The famous nineteenth-century naturalist Frank Buckland wrote in his *Curiosities of Natural History*, second series, of how he had personally inspected the Waterloo Bridge bones. Himself a doctor, he was able to conclude that the cuts had been made by someone accustomed to handling a saw, but with no knowledge of anatomy. He also held that a woman and a black cat were somehow mixed up in the affair, for he and the great microscopist Professor Quekett found the hairs of both sticking to the remains. The perpetrator of that crime was never brought to book.

Meanwhile, returning to 1873, back at Battersea the police were netting and dragging the river, and scouring its banks. They continued to do so until darkness fell on the Saturday (6 September).

Shortly after the finding of the left quarter of the torso of the mutilated woman, Henry Locke, a policeman in the employ of the South-Western Railway Company, was on duty. That Friday morning (5 September), at Brunswick Wharf, Nine Elms, around 10.30 a.m., he was walking along the wharf on the Thames front when he saw something floating in the water some six or so yards from the wharf wall. He thought that it was part of a sheepskin, and threw several stones at it, but as it floated by Locke clambered on to a passing barge and asked the bargee to hook it up with a boathook. When he took the object off the boathook he found it was a female breast, which he hurriedly put into a bag before sending for a policeman, who came and took it away and gave it into the custody of Inspector Starkey of the Thames Police. It was subsequently conveyed to Battersea Police Station, where Dr Felix Charles Kempster duly examined it.

At 6.45 on the morning of Saturday 6th, PC John Parker of the Thames Police noticed a small crowd of people clustered on the Duke shore, at Limehouse. They were looking at something in the water, close to the shore. What was intriguing them was a face, or rather the peeled-off skin of a face. It was obvious at a glance that the murderer or murderers had taken revolting precautions to prevent identification. The eyes had been taken out, but one eyebrow remained. The nose had been cut off through the cartilage, but was still hanging attached to the upper lip. There were several cuts on the mouth. There was no jawbone. Both ears were there. It had obviously been carried down by the tide and deposited in the eddy above the pier. Parker bore it off to Wapping Police Station, but was sent on with it to Inspector Charles Marley on the *Royalist*. Marley delivered it into the hands of the detectives at Scotland Yard.

Thence it was taken to the Clapham and Wandsworth Union Workhouse, where, in the mortuary, all the discovered remains were stored, and where Dr Kempster, summarising his conclusions, stated that the first find had been the left-hand side and thorax of a female, perfectly fresh, and that in his opinion death had occurred not many hours before. The breast, very full and uninjured, was that of a woman of about forty years of age. He had found no portion of the viscera, except for a small remnant of the diaphragm, and the heart and lungs were missing. The body had been separated between the second and third vertebrae above the spinal column, and divided from the lower part immediately before the fourth rib. The ribs had been cut through at the back, partially through the spinal column. The arm had been removed at the middle of the clavicle, all of the shoulder having been taken away. In Kempster's opinion a knife and a fine saw had been used. The blood vessels were entirely empty and there were no integuments. The muscles were no doubt divided immediately after death, and that was when the body was cut up.

At about 2 p.m. the same day Kempster saw the right side of the same body – exactly matching the left-hand quarter. It was separated from the other portion, but when he put them together they formed part of the same body. There was none of the viscera attached to the second half. On the chest was a large white scar, the result of a burn, probably in childhood, and there was a very small mole on the right-hand side of the neck. To all appearances the body was that of a perfectly healthy woman.

The Lancet elaborated:

There is very strong evidence that the woman met with a violent death, and that in the first instance severe blows were dealt on the right side of the head with some heavy blunt instrument; but, in the absence of the skull, it is impossible to determine positively the extent of the injury. It would appear that after the victim had been stunned the body was immediately deprived of all its blood by a section of the carotid arteries in the neck, since there were no clots in any of the veins of the body.

The scalp and skin of the face were probably next removed by making a longitudinal incision through the scalp at the top of the head and a horizontal incision behind. The skin and pericranial tissues were then drawn forcibly forward and the skull thus laid bare, occasional touches of the knife being necessary to remove the skin of the face. Where the integument was thin or firmly adhered to the subjacent tissues it was 'button holed', and large portions thus remained attached to the bones.

The upper part of the nose is absent, as well as the inner part of the left cheek and the lower lip and chin, all of which would have required some time for their removal.

Contrary to the popular opinion, the body has not been hacked, but dexterously cut up; the joints have been opened, and the bones neatly disarticulated, even the complicated joints at the ankle and the elbow, and it is only at the articulations of the hip-joint and shoulder that the bones have been sawn through. In the trunk the sections have all been made in the most favourable parts. This is clearly shown on the left side of the trunk, for after the body had been divided longitudinally, the right side was severed into three portions, a thoracic, an abdominal and a pelvic. To make these divisions, an incision had been commenced too high, and the knife coming in contact with the lower part of the costal arch, a fresh incision was therefore made lower down, in order to clear the ribs.

We fear that identification is next to impossible, except to those who are accurately acquainted with the very few marks which the body presents – namely, a scar as of a burn on the thorax, which, however, is very common in girls and women; a small prominent fibroma, which in the official description of the body is said to be a pale mole, on the inner side of the right nipple; and the cicatrix over the inner condyle of the right femur. It is not a little remarkable, however, that although the right leg between the knee and the ankle is perfect, on the left side the leg has been sawn in two, and only the upper part has been found. It is possible that there may have been some mark on the lower portion of this leg which the murderer has taken the precaution to destroy. The hands also are unfortunately missing.

It appears that much importance is attached to the evidence of the woman recently having had a child or not; and although the uterus is very small and firm, and the areolae around the nipples are pale, it would be well to have this part of the question carefully reconsidered.

It is clear, then, that this is not a practical joke, and such an hypothesis must appear preposterous if, in addition to the evidence that the death was a violent one, it is borne in mind that the body bears no trace of dissection, or of having been used for operative surgery; for although we have said that the bones have been skilfully disarticulated, it is in a manner different from what obtains in the performance of any operation, for there are no flaps. Farther, there is the distinct statement of the Inspector of Anatomy that no body was given out by him for anatomical purposes during the week in which the mutilated remains of this woman were discovered; so that no body could have been obtained from any of the dissecting rooms, all of which are indeed at present closed.

The Lancet was to comment further:

The public has, happily, in the course of thirty years learnt to dissociate the medical student and the Burker, who may now be fairly said to be extinct. But, as recent events seem to show, there is still a tendency to make the student the scape-goat of any horrid murder or frightful mutilations. This is to be regretted for more reasons than one, but chiefly because it interferes with the course of justice, by leading it off its proper track.

As time moved on, a public rumour gradually shaped itself into a widely held belief that one Mrs Cailey, a widow, who had been missing for some time from her Chelsea home, was the dismembered woman.

She fitted the doctors' profile. She was described as 'Age: 40. Height: 5ft. 8 in. Well made. Inclined to stoutness. Thin aquiline nose. Small ears. Dark hair. Soft, dark down on upper lip forming a moustache. Dress when last seen: Black dress and bonnet, with white rose. Grey jacket with black buttons. Red petticoat. Side-spring boots.' Moreover, it was bruited abroad that several people who had actually seen the body recognised it as that of Mrs Cailey.

An important witness, Mary Ann Christian, testified:

I am married, and my husband is a traveller. I live at 15 South Street, Battersea Park, and have one or two ladies to board and lodge with me. Of late I have only had one. A person named Cailey came up from Dorsetshire at the beginning of August this year, to stay for a week until her affairs were settled. She told me she was thirty-three, but she looked older than that, nearer forty. She said she had come up to get her property, and all her affairs settled; that her husband had sold his cottages. She said she had to see her solicitor, Mr Thompson, a solicitor in Lincoln's Inn. No female joined her at my house, but she had a bed and bedroom to herself.

I last saw her alive on 2 September. She left my house at ten o'clock, with the intention of getting her things out of pledge, as she told me, and she was to receive some money from her solicitor, as her property was to be divided into three parts. She used to be out till eleven o'clock, and I call that late for a woman.

She was shabbily dressed. The skirt was of Coburg, but the bodice was separate. She had a grey jacket bound with black, and black buttons of imitation jet. I had spoken to her of her late habits, but I never saw her the worse for drink. On her return home I never noticed the condition of her clothes at any time. She showed me the mark of a bruise, which she said she had received the night before. It was on her temple. Her hair was short, dark, and very thin. She wore a plait of hair at the side of her face, and a black net bonnet. She showed me the bruise quite a week or more before the last time I saw her. I never saw her again in the company of anyone. She always told me she was out about her property. I never saw her undressed, or any marks on her person. She never had any letters, but said she had an intimate friend in Paulton Square, who kept a number of rabbits or cats.

I have seen the scalp and face. I firmly believe the face I have seen is that of Mrs Cailey. She was a tall woman – about 5ft. 8¾ inches. She paid me 2s.6d. deposit when she came, and that is all I have had. I found her in food. I was to have written to her brother, but did not do so, as she spoke to me about her affairs and seemed in a great deal of trouble. She knew so many people in London, that I thought she was a very respectable person. She had no boxes, but said they were all at Paulton Square. She used to go to her friend there to change her clothes.

The suspicion of the police that the mutilated body was not that of Mrs Cailey turned out to be correct. On Wednesday morning, 17 September, the persistence of the police in their searching for Mrs Cailey paid off. Who should the detectives spot in a street off the King's Road, walking along gaily and looking 'in the pink', but Mrs Cailey. Later that Wednesday, Mrs Cailey met her relatives at the house in South Street, where she had formerly lodged. On being questioned as to the reason why she had not come forward, and so avoided the attention of the public and saved the time of the police, she said that she had been to Scotland with a gentleman, and that she had been so horrified by the story of the murder in the Thames that she had refused to read about it or to listen to any account of it.

A piece of information channelled to the police was that there was aboard a particular barge a woman whose husband or paramour, the bargee, was known to be of a volcanically violent disposition. This man and the woman worked the barge together, and she was commonly to be seen going about her barge-board jobs. She, dark, stout, aged about forty, matched the doctors' description of the anonymous victim. The barge had been at Battersea on Wednesday (3 September), when it discharged a cargo, and on Thursday (4th) evening took in another cargo. She left on Friday morning – the morning on which the remains were found down the river. The barge was seen by a number of bargemen, but of the woman there was, unusually, no sign. She was later discovered unharmed.

A final disappointment followed upon the failure of what had seemed like the strong claim of a Mrs Carter that the remains of the woman found at Battersea were those of her daughter.

Mrs Carter, the widow of a railway platelayer, residing in the village of Moyland, near Maldon, called upon Inspector Rutledge and told him that she had every reason to believe that the parts of the body found in the Thames were those of her daughter, Mary Ann, who had been in service near Clapham Common before disappearing without a trace. The woman, who was plainly in great distress, stated to the inspector that, in Mary Ann's last letter to her, her daughter had expressed her intention of bettering her conditions, although she did not say in what way. Mrs Carter had written to Mary Ann several times, but, not getting an answer to any of her letters, asked two of her sisters in London to make inquiries. Mrs Carter had heard nothing to relieve her suspense until Monday (8 September), when she read the particulars of the Thames murder, and she at once came to the conclusion that her daughter was the victim. Upon receipt of this information, Inspector Rutledge immediately communicated with Superintendent Williams of the Detective Department at Scotland Yard.

Mrs Carter applied again to Inspector Rutledge. He read out to her the description of the body found, and when he came to the bit about the mole on the neck Mrs Carter exclaimed, 'Oh, my poor daughter had a mole on her neck.' Reading on, the inspector came to the scar on the forearm. Said Mrs Carter, 'It is my daughter. My poor daughter.' In answer to Rutledge, she said that her daughter had a large scar on that part of her arm, adding that the description of the nose and colour of the hair was quite similar to those of her daughter. Inspector Rutledge again communicated with Superintendent Williams, detailing all the particulars which had transpired. Upon investigation, Mary Ann Carter was found alive and well, living in Clapham.

The trail thus went cold.

In May 1961, not long before we moved into a top-floor flat – No. 32 – at Albert Mansions, in Albert Bridge Road, a murder was committed at Albert Studios, a row of small mews cottages, once the stable quarters, situated at the back of, and serving, the mansions. Well into the advanced evening of Sunday 7 May the telephone rang in the Elm Park Road, Chelsea, home of Dr Richard Castillo, who was on rota duty that weekend, covering for his colleague, Dr David Craig, of Oakley Street, Chelsea.

The call, taken by his daughter, Angela, was from a man who, giving the name of Allenby, said that he was a patient of Dr Craig's. 'Will the doctor come and see my wife?' he asked. 'She is sick with blood.' He gave the address of Albert Studios, Albert Bridge Road. The man had, said Angela, a foreign voice.

Dr Castillo took his bag and drove across Albert Bridge and down to the small private road that turned off opposite Battersea Park and led to the back of Albert Mansions. Fitfully lamplit, heavily tree-shrouded, it was an eerie ambush into which Dr Castillo had been lured.

As time ticked on and there was no sign of Dr Castillo's returning home, his wife became worried, agitated. She telephoned Dr Craig. He said that he had no patient by the name of Allenby, and none living at Albert Studios. He would, he said, investigate.

Dr Craig drove to Albert Studios. And there, on the bosky path, lit by a single, rather feeble, lamp, lay the doctor. He had been viciously struck down, stabbed to death.

Thomas Vaughan Welsh, singer and actor, occupant of No. 2 Albert Studios, said that he had heard an outcry – 'It was rather a terrifying noise' – and, looking out, saw an elderly man struggling on the edge of a patch of light. And Patrick John Furse, an artist, also of Albert Studios, said, 'I saw someone knock on the door of No. 3, next door to mine. They knocked two or three times, apparently getting no reply.' He then heard someone 'calling incoherently'.

Dr Castillo, who was seventy-one, was born on the island of Malta; he had been practising in Chelsea since 1923, and was very well liked.

A third doctor, Ivan Weisz, emerges upon the scene. Born in Czechoslovakia in 1917, he qualified medically there and was in private practice for a short time before being sent, in 1942, by the Germans, to a labour camp in the Ukraine. Severely injured during bombing by the Allied forces, he escaped to Romania and went to Egypt. Following a period in a refugee camp, he came to England in 1949. He qualified here in 1955, and his name was duly entered on the Medical Register.

After holding various hospital appointments, he became, in June 1957, a trainee assistant to Dr Castillo.

He left Dr Castillo in June 1958, saying that he had got on with him 'on good terms as employer and employee'. He agreed that during September, October, November and December 1960, the first four months in which he had set up in practice on his own account in King's Road, Chelsea, sixty-one patients had transferred from Dr Castillo's list to his, but he emphasised that they did so of their own free will.

However, on 16 February 1961, Dr Castillo made a formal complaint to the General Medical Council, and notice was given to Dr Weisz. One year later, in February 1962, Dr Weisz, of Avonmore, Viewfield Road, S.W., found himself before the disciplinary committee accused of infamous conduct in a professional respect, canvassing patients, and deprecating the professional skill, knowledge and services of Dr Castillo.

In May 1961, Dr Castillo had been murdered.

In February 1962, the GMC ordered Dr Weisz's name to be struck from the Medical Register.

The murder was never solved. Is the third of this medical trinity, one wonders, the unholy ghost?

Part Two
The Floaters of Death

To begin, as Dylan Thomas was fain portentously to intone, at the beginning, we must needs travel a dozen or so miles to the north-east of Battersea, to what was, 128 years ago, the historic Essex village of Rainham, and is now a suburban town in east London, part of the Greater London borough of Havering.

Here, on the morning of 11 May 1887, lighterman Edward Henry Hughes is foursquare aboard his flat-bottomed barge or lighter, whereon he earns his daily bread conveying goods from mid-river ships to adjacent shoreline factories, such as Frederick Hempleman's, producing fertiliser compounded of the noisome elements of blood and fish; one of several factories feelingly described thereabouts as 'obnoxious', because of the odours which they imperviously cast upon the air. This morning, however, Hughes's nostrils remain unperturbed, for his seafaring eye is caught and focussed upon a bobbing alien object which he has espied floating in the water.

It is a bulky, coarse sack. Hughes adroitly hooks it and hauls it in. Then, prising apart the sodden sackcloth – shock, horror! – there is revealed the pallid, waterlogged torso of a woman.

A policeman was eagerly sought and found. Police Constable Stock, of the Essex constabulary, carried the sack and its gruesome contents away, and deposited it in a shed hard by the Phoenix Hotel, in Rainham, there to await further examination. That examination was undertaken by Dr Edward Galloway, who was the police surgeon of nearby Barking. Noting that the torso had been sawn through with a very fine, sharp saw, the muscle cut clean with a sweet-edged knife, the thighs skilfully disarticulated from the pelvic sockets and the spine severed at precisely the spot where it proved least resistant, Galloway decided that the dissection had been carried out by somebody possessed of an intimate knowledge of the anatomical techniques of surgery.

The corpse was that of a woman of between twenty-seven and twenty-nine years of age; although she could possibly have been as old as thirty-five. Her probable height would have been five feet and three inches, or five feet and four inches. Her hair, Galloway thought to have been brown. By his reckoning, she had been dead for about two weeks.

And that is just about all that was ever discovered about the anonymous victim. On 3 June the inquest jury returned an open verdict, and the murder was filed away, unsolved, labelled the Rainham Mystery.

But the Rainham affair was to initiate the onset of a series of neatly packaged floaters in the Thames, which lasted from 1887 until 1889, and sowed the seed of a notion that a riverine Jack the Ripper was at knife-plying work.

It was a couple of days after the inquest on the Rainham cadaver, that is on Sunday 5 June 1887, at ten o'clock in the morning, that another Thames-side worker, pier worker J. Morris, encountered another floating package – a large parcel in the water, near the lower side of Temple Pier, which was situated halfway between Blackfriars and Waterloo Bridges. Morris dragged it out, intrepidly tore it open, and drew forth a human thigh, wrapped in sacking. The Thames Police were hastily summoned, and the thigh was borne away, to be submitted to Dr Galloway, who exhibited no hesitation in confirming that it emanated from the Rainham body. The thigh was despatched to the City mortuary, but Mr Samuel Frederick Langham, the City coroner, refused to hold an inquest on it, pointing out that the law stated that only a vital part of a body could be the subject of a coroner's inquiry. So the thigh was slipped into a pauper's pinewood coffin and interred at the City of London Cemetery, at Little Ilford. In due course both the thigh and the Rainham torso, which latter had been buried in Rainham churchyard, were exhumed.

A second discovery that Sunday (5 June) was that of a woman's chest, bereft of breasts. It was found on the foreshore at Battersea Park. At half-past three on 30 June, a boy approached Francis Thurle, lock-keeper at the St Pancras Lock, to tell him that a human arm had been pulled out of the Regent's Canal and was on the towpath. Thurle made his way there, took possession of the arm, and carted it off to the mortuary.

The next morning, 1 July, a labourer named Perry found another arm at the same place, and that afternoon George Mansfield, a labourer in the employ of the Regent's Canal Company, handed over to the police two legs which he said that he had found in the canal. Dr Galloway went to St Pancras Mortuary, inspected the four limbs, and declared that they all belonged to the Rainham torso. The doctor said that, except for the head and upper part of the chest, the entire body of the Rainham victim was now in the possession of the police.

An inquest was opened at the Crowndale Hall, in Camden Town, on 11 July 1887. It was presided over by Dr G. Danford Thomas, the coroner for Central Middlesex. After evidence had been heard from Dr Galloway, the coroner announced that the Home Secretary, Henry Matthews, had ordered a more detailed examination of the remains, and that the inquiry would therefore be adjourned until 6 August.

Dr Thomas Bond, surgeon at the Westminster Hospital and the police divisional surgeon to A Division (Whitehall), was requested to examine all the remains – eleven separate body parts. This he did, assisted by Dr Charles Alfred Hebbert, a colleague of his at the Westminster Hospital, and came to the same conclusion as Galloway – that the murderer displayed definite anatomical skill.

The doctors reported that the ovaries were small and the *rugae* of the vagina prominent, indicating that this was a woman who had never given birth. The pubic hair

was black and an incision had been made in the vaginal
wall's cartilage. There was no sign of bruising near any
of the incisions, which proved that dismemberment had
been done quickly, and soon after death. Since there
was no ring indentation on either hand, the woman had
probably been unmarried. The state of the bones was
indicative of an age of over twenty-five years. Grooves
below the knees suggested that garters had been worn.
This provided a hint as regards the social position of the
woman, for it was the more common custom among
the lower orders to wear garters below the knees. The
upper classes wore either garters *above* the knees, or,
alternatively, suspenders.

Dr Danford Thomas's inquest was concluded on 13
August. Bereft as they were of any really significant data,
the best verdict that the jury could manage was 'Found
dead'.

Sixteen months were to pass before evidence came
floating into view that the unknown murderer had been
at it again. Around 12.45 p.m. on Tuesday 11 September
1888, Frederick Moore, standing by the gates of Ward's
Deal Wharf – 113 Grosvenor Road – where he was
employed, saw a gathered knot of workmen looking in
some excitement over the embankment, near the sluices
from Messrs Seager, Evans & Co.'s Millbank distillery, at
something entangled in a raft of floating timber. Moore
went over and joined the group. They were saying that
the object was, without question, a human arm. Moore
did not agree. One of the men went and fetched a ladder,
and, as the tide was going out, Moore went down to
take a closer look. The men were right; it was an arm.
Moore disentangled it from the timber's grasp, pulled it
out of the water, and laid it on the bank upon another
timber's handy bed. The arm was naked, that is to say
that it was not wrapped in anything, but Moore noticed
that there was a piece of string which had been tied
very tightly round its upper part. Having first made a

thorough search through the surrounding mud for any further stray bits of human anatomy, and finding none, Moore clambered back up the ladder and trotted off in search of a policeman. He found PC William James on duty on Grosvenor Embankment. James duly took the arm into custody, and conveyed it into the safekeeping of Superintendent Shepherd at Gerald Street Police Station.

Shepherd immediately called in the acting divisional surgeon, Dr Thomas Neville, who lived at 85 Pimlico Road and practised at 23 Sloane Street. After a careful scrutiny he pronounced it to be the right arm of a woman, which had been in the water no more than two or three days. Because its muscles were not much contracted, he thought the arm must have been cut off post-mortem – cleanly severed with an adequately sharp knife.

Dr Hebbert performed a confirmatory examination on the following Sunday (16 September). He also found it to be a female right arm, measuring thirty-one inches in circumference at the shoulder, and six and a half inches at the wrist. The hand measured seven and a half inches long, and the nails were small and well shaped. He also thought that the arm had been separated from the shoulder joint after death, and that the dissection had been executed by someone who, although not an anatomist, was familiar with the joints, and well knew what he was doing.

Street gossip began to take sinister shape. Commented *The Echo*:

> The wildest rumours are already afloat as to whether another hideous crime, even more mysterious than the Whitechapel murders, has or has not been perpetrated in the West-end of London. There are believed to be some startling features in connection with the case which cannot at present be revealed, as officials are now engaged in making their investigation into this, the latest London mystery.

Speculatively, *The Echo* went on to report that the arm was that of a woman 'killed by the same unseen hand that committed the dastardly crimes in Whitechapel,' and that the arm had eventually 'been brought from the East-end to Pimlico, in order to throw the police off the scent. Inspector Abberline, Inspector Helson, Inspector Reid, and other officers engaged in investigating the Whitechapel crimes have been in communication with Scotland Yard with reference to the finding of the arm, but no clue has yet been found.'

The next discovery was made by a fourteen-year-old boy walking to work along the Lambeth Road, at half-past seven on the morning of Friday 28 September 1888. As he passed the Blind School, the garden of which, surrounded by staunch iron railings, faced on to the road, he spied lying there a parcel. Curious, as boys will be, and wrestling with the difficulty created by the railings, the lad contrived to drag the parcel out between its iron teeth. Upon eagerly tearing it open, he was alarmed, surprised and disappointed in equal measure to find that, instead of the anticipated treasure, the mystery parcel contained a human arm.

Unbeknown to the boy, all along he had been under the observation of a watchful-eyed bricklayer named Moore, who now scampered off as fast as his legs would carry him to inform the policeman, whom he knew to be on fixed-point duty nearby, of what had been found. Moore then plunged into the Crown and Grapes, directly across the road from the Blind School, to apprise the assemblage therein that some 'Leather Apron' tricks were going on over the road.

One of the aforesaid assemblage, a Mr William George Davis, popped out in time to see a policeman bearing off a bundle, wrapped about with coarse brown material, a portion of which had been ripped away, permitting of the display of a wrist and hand with strangely curled fingers. It was taken to Kennington Lane Police Station.

William Allen, licensed shoeblack, whose pitch was outside the Crown and Grapes, thought that the arm within the parcel, of which he had caught a glimpse, had been laid in lime. He also maintained that it had not been where it was found for much more than an hour, because the road sweepers had passed that very spot an hour or so before and had not seen it. They would assuredly have registered it had it been there.

Unbelievably, on 2 October 1888, a human torso came to light in, of all unexpected places, the vaults at Scotland Yard. The vaults were actually those of the New Scotland Yard building, which was under construction on the Thames-side site which had originally been chosen for the National Opera House, a fiscally overreaching enterprise which bankrupted its promoter, Colonel James Henry Mapleson. Sold off after the collapse of the National Opera House project and the demolition of the portion of the building already erected, the site was subsequently purchased by the government and Richard Norman Shaw's red-and-white coloured, seven-storey building was scheduled to be ready for occupation by the Metropolitan Police in 1889.

The discovery of the torso was made by Frederick Wildbore, a carpenter in the employ of the Pimlico firm of J. Grove & Sons, who were one of the contractors working on the building. At 6 a.m. on Monday 1 October 1888, Wildbore went into the vault to collect his tools. It should be explained that some of the workmen had had their tools stolen, so it had become the custom for them to hide them away when they finished work on a Saturday in this particular vault – thirty feet long, twenty-four feet wide, twelve feet deep, laid over above with loose planking.

The place was pitch-dark, and Wildbore struck a match. In its brief flare he saw what he thought was an old coat rolled up in the recess where his tools had been hidden. The following day he and several of his workmates made a closer inspection of the bundle. One of them, George Budgen, said, 'I looked at it and found all the top of it bare, the rest being wrapped up in some old cloth. I thought it was old bacon at first, thrown away there, or something of that sort, but as I could make nothing of it, I took hold of the strings round it and dragged it out into the light. I then got my pocket knife and dragged the strings off it.'

Budgen, Wildbore and half a dozen others gazed in stunned silence at the revealed headless, armless, legless torso of an obviously murdered woman, and one of them, Charlie Brown, hared off to King Street Police Station, where, as registered by the station clock, he arrived panting and breathless at 3.20 p.m. After listening to his tale, the inspector in charge assigned a detective, Thomas Hawkins, to go straight off to the building site. He was followed there shortly afterwards by Dr Thomas Bond, who, after a cursory inspection, ordered the torso to be removed to the mortuary, where he and Dr Hebbert conducted a joint examination of the New Scotland Yard remains.

They reported,

Torso 17 inches long. 35½ inches around the chest, 28½ inches at the waist. Breasts large and prominent. Appearance of collar-bones indicate woman of mature development, certainly over 24 or 25 years of age. Fair skin. Dark hair. Full fleshed and well nourished. Height: about 5 feet 8 inches. Does not appear to have borne a child. Died between six weeks and two months ago. Neither suffocated nor drowned. Body badly decomposed, especially where the head and limbs had been removed. No wounds that could have been the cause of death revealed. Inside of the heart pale and free from clots. [Even so, Bond thought death likely to have been due to haemorrhage or fainting.] The head had been removed from the trunk by sawing through

the sixth cervical vertebra. The neck had been divided
by several jagged incisions at the bottom of the larynx,
which had been sawn through. The lower limbs and
pelvis had been removed with a series of long, sweeping
cuts with a saw through the lumbar vertebrae, and the
arms had been removed at the shoulder joints by several
oblique downward incisions, carried round the arms and
straight through the joints. The body appeared to have
been wrapped up in a very skilful manner, the wrapping
so securely tied that over the body there were clearly
defined marks where the strings had been. The stomach,
liver and kidneys were normal. The left lung was healthy,
but the left lung was firmly adherent to the chest wall of
the diaphragm, indicating that at some time the woman
had suffered from severe pleurisy. The stomach contained
about an ounce of partly digested food. The uterus was
absent.

Apropos the cording used to bind the package up, it was,
according to the inquest evidence of Inspector Marshall,
a mixture of string, one piece of sash-cord and a piece of
black tape. As to the wrapping material, it was a piece of
a dress of broche satin cloth.

The torso must have weighed all of fifty pounds –
quite a considerable weight for even a strong man to
carry for any distance. Added to that was the problem
of how the killer could have negotiated himself and the
heavy burden over the seven- or eight-foot hoarding by
which the site was surrounded.

Investigation disclosed three possible entrances to the
site – two in Cannon Row, one from the Embankment.
The Embankment entrance did not seem a very practical
one because, being open and unprotected, it presented
a very considerable risk of being seen; Cannon Row on
the other hand, despite being almost opposite the Home
Office in Parliament Street, was a dark and distinctly
lonely spot. Whatever the source of ingress, someone had

either climbed on to the iron pillar that stood beside the hoarding or discovered the small gate in Cannon Row, which was unlocked and fastened only with a catch that was lifted by pulling a piece of string.

The likelihood would seem to be that the torso had been dumped by someone who was well acquainted with the site; perhaps a current or previous employee. Moreover, the body could only have been placed where it was found between Saturday night and the early hours of Monday morning, because at three o'clock on Friday afternoon Charlie Brown had been in the vault along with several other men, and at 4.40 p.m. on the Saturday, Ernest Hedge, left alone on the site to lock up, had gone into the vault to get a hammer and was unshakeably certain that there had been no torso there then – 'I was in the very corner where the parcel was discovered.'

On 17 October Jasper Waring, a London journalist, brought his black Russian terrier, Smoker, to the vault. Practically immediately it showed signs of having the scent of something underground. The earth was carefully removed and, at a depth of less than six inches, the dog seized what turned out to be a human foot. A little further away, buried at a depth of about twelve inches, they found an arm.

Dr Bond was smartly summoned. He saw the partially buried leg and opined that the soil yielded unmistakable evidence of having covered the leg for at least several weeks. Both he and Hebbert harboured no doubts that the arm and the leg belonged to the body in the bundle. And Bond was now more convinced than ever that, despite the assertions of Ernest Hedge and others, the torso must have been where it was found for quite some time. 'I took,' he said, 'the opportunity to examine the spot where the body was found, and I am quite sure that Hedge is wrong as to the body not having been there a few days before. The body must have lain there for weeks, and it had decomposed there.'

Bond explained: 'The brickwork against which it had leant was deeply covered with the decomposed fluid of the human body turned black, and it could not have done that in a day or two. The stain is not superficial, but the brickwork is quite saturated. I should think it must have been there quite six weeks when found – from August. Also the earth beneath it had sunk, indicating that the load of the torso had rested on it for a long time.'

On the afternoon of 8 October, Mr John Troutbeck, the deputy coroner for Westminster, had opened the inquest in the Westminster Sessions House, Broad Sanctuary. Having taken testimony from several witnesses, however, he adjourned the inquiry for two weeks.

The inquest reopened on 22 October, and, after hearing more testimony, the coroner summed up, concluding that there was no evidence as to the identity of the woman or the cause of death. It was to be supposed that the dissection indicated that she had been murdered, but it was for the jury to decide whether the verdict should be 'Found dead' or 'Wilful murder against some person unknown'.

The jury consulted briefly and returned the verdict of 'Found dead'.

On the warm, sunlit Tuesday morning of 4 June 1889, fifteen-year-old Isaac Brett, who lived at No. 7 Lawrence Street, in Chelsea, and earned his living as a woodcutter, was walking along the Battersea foreshore, just under the Albert Bridge, when he decided to take a dip. Barely had he entered the water when he saw a package, all neatly tied up with a bootlace, floating by. He grasped hold of it and took it ashore. Young Brett did not open it, but, acting upon the advice offered by a passing stranger, bore the package off to Battersea Police Station, where Sergeant William Briggs of V Division opened it. It contained a thigh, wrapped in a torn length of a woman's chequer-patterned ulster overcoat. Also contained within the package was the right leg of a pair of women's drawers, on the waistband of which, written in black ink, was the name L. E. FISHER.

Dr Felix Charles Kempster, the Battersea divisional police surgeon, was called in, as was Dr Thomas Bond. Kempster's findings on the thigh were that it had not been in the water long, and that death had occurred only twenty-four hours earlier, which gave a murder date – if indeed it was murder – of Monday 3 June. He also identified four bruise marks on the thigh. These, he said, were almost certainly the consequence of a firm grip applied to the limb, and were caused while the victim was alive.

An inquest was held by Wynne E. Baxter, the coroner of East Middlesex, who, incidentally, presided over the inquests of alleged Ripper victims Polly Nichols, Annie Chapman and Liz Stride. Most unsatisfactorily, however, the evidence as it stood could not decisively establish whether a murder had been committed.

Joseph Davis, employed as a gardener in Battersea Park, was inoffensively pursuing his quiet work near the wrought-iron fence which divides the park from the river, a couple of hundred yards from the nearest gate, at Albert Bridge, on the afternoon of 6 June 1889 when he came upon a bundle. It was lying, innocent-looking, amid the greenery of the rhododendron shrubbery. It was, he noted, neatly tied up with white venetian blind cord. Upon opening it, Davis dropped the thing in shock, horrified to recognise parcelled therein bits and pieces of a human body. Off he shot in a desperate dash in search of one of the patrolling park policemen. He found Constable 502 Walter Ainger of V Division, and the pair of them agreed that what was in that horrible parcel was the upper part of a dead woman. It was wrapped in a burgundy-coloured skirt.

Later that same day, in Battersea Mortuary, the divisional police surgeon examined Davis's find and reported:

The chest cavity was empty, but many internal organs including the spleen, both kidneys, and a portion of the stomach and intestines, were present. The lower six dorsal vertebrae were in their place, but the lower five ribs were missing. A portion of the midriff above the breasts and the integumentary covering to the chest-bone were cut down the centre as though by a saw. The ribs were also sawn through. Decomposition had set in, but had proceeded no further than was consistent with the assumption that the remains formed part of a living body not more than four or at the most five days previously.

If the doctor was correct about that, then the murder might have taken place as early as 2 June.

A short time before Joseph Davis's unpleasant find among the rhododendrons, Charles Marlow, a barge builder who lived in Wye Street, Battersea, while at work at Covington Wharf, Battersea, spotted a strange object in the water. He reported it to the police. Inspector William Law of the Thames Division took possession of it at Waterloo Pier, a station relatively near Temple Pier, where part of the Rainham body had been found two years before.

Further body parts turned up near Palace Wharf, at Nine Elms, Battersea. They were found by an engineer named David Keen. And there was even more to come. Solomon Hearne was one of a community of gypsies who, at that time, lived on the bank of the Thames, camping on the open shore in summer and dossing in winter in the bankside rookeries before their demolition to make way for Joseph Bazalgette's Embankment. Hearne had struck camp in Fulham, at Lammas Land, by Two Meadows, just east of Wandsworth Bridge, and it was there that he found, lying on the foreshore, a woman's leg. It was wrapped in the collar of a chequered ulster identical to the piece in which the thigh found by Isaac Brett near Albert Bridge had been wrapped.

At Battersea Mortuary, Dr Kempster, religiously following what had now become his routine procedure, preserved the limb in spirits of wine. He also confirmed that the leg, which had been cut off just below the knee, belonged to the same body as that which had been yielding the other jigsaw fragments.

Two further pieces would be found on 7 June, when David Goodman, a nitric acid maker, of 15 Prairie Street, Queen's Road, Battersea, came upon a piece of flesh lying on the mud at Palace Wharf, and lighterman Edward Stanton, of Park Street, Limehouse, caught sight of a dark bundle floating in the water of the West India Docks. The bundle was tied with string. The material of which it was externally composed was the chequered ulster's sleeve. The parcel was passed to Inspector Hodson of the Thames Division, who duly passed it on to Dr Kempster, who confirmed that its contents – a right leg and foot – belonged to the same female body.

Another lighterman, William Chidley, at work at 8 a.m. on Saturday 8 June at Bankside, Southwark, hauled ashore a floating package, wrapped in plain brown paper. In it nestled a woman's severed left arm, concerning which Kempster reported that 'the limb was well moulded and the hand small and shaped with every appearance of having been well cared for. The arm had been severed from the body in a very skilled manner, and the person who cut it off must have had a very considerable knowledge of anatomy.' It bore a small scar on the forearm.

The police themselves produced the next body part. At half-past twelve that same Saturday (8 June), an object was observed midstream between Battersea Park Pier and the Albert Suspension Bridge. Although modesty might well have demanded it, there was no wrapping around the naked buttocks, pelvis and lower back thus exposed, which Sub-Inspector Joseph Churcher carried off, impervious, to the Battersea mortuary.

The third discovery dispensed by that generous 8 June was made by Claude Mellor, a journalist. He had been assigned to the torso story by his paper, *The Star*, and at midday was wandering bemusedly, and story-wise befoggedly, along Chelsea Embankment, wondering what on earth he was going to write. Passing just then a seductive line of evergreens skirting the railings that edged the gardens of a rich man's acres, he noticed, with the journalist's acuity, something somewhat hidden in the undergrowth. Having hailed beat-plodding PC 182B Jones, Mellor took him back to what turned out to be the home of Sir Percy Shelley, descendent of Mary, creator of *Frankenstein*, and there, wrapped in a telltale tear-off of the chequered ulster, lay a much decomposed right thigh.

The matching right arm and hand were found by lighterman Joseph Squire, floating in the Thames at Newton's Wharf, by Bankside, near Blackfriars Bridge.

Drs Bond, Kempster and Hebbert foregathered at Battersea Mortuary on 10 June.

Hebbert in his report first lists the parts found – two large flaps of skin from the abdominal walls and right buttock, the uterus and placenta, both arms and hands, both thighs, both legs and feet, the trunk, divided into three parts. Only missing was the all-important head. The top portion of the trunk had been removed from the head at the sixth vertebra by a series of clean, confident cuts. The chest had been opened in front by the midline, the sternum cut through and the contents of the chest (lungs and heart) removed. The arms had been removed by three or four long, sweeping cuts, the joints neatly disarticulated. The skin was peeling off in places from the sodden flesh, but the portion had not been in the water long. The second section of the trunk contained both breasts and fitted exactly with the first, including the vertical cut through the sternum. The ribs were present and, although the intestines had gone, the kidneys, spleen, pancreas and liver were still in place, along with the duodenum and part of the stomach. Despite decomposition of the liver, all the internal organs were healthy. The final part of the trunk showed that the thighs had been removed by those same long, sweeping incisions and here was the same skilful disarticulation of the joints. The pelvis contained the lower part of the vagina and rectum and the front part of the bladder, including the urethra. The vagina itself showed no damage, either from violent rape or childbirth. The skin was fair and the pubic hair a light sandy colour. The uterus had been cut, but the existence of the placenta and the organ's dilation made it clear that the woman had been pregnant and the foetus removed by her killer. The dead woman would have been between six or seven months pregnant. Indentations on a finger of the left hand implied a wedding ring. A number of circular scars on the upper left arm indicated vaccination. There was a small scar on the lower forearm. The leg sections fitted perfectly, with no deformities to the feet. The woman's age was likely to be over twenty-four years, probably under thirty-five.

Hebbert's best calculation as to her height was just shy of five feet and five inches. Dr Bond said that, because the neck and stomach were missing, he was unable to say if the woman's throat had been cut or if lethal drugs had been administered to her. There was no way that he could determine the cause of death.

A rather odd discovery had been that of a piece of fine linen, measuring some nine inches by eight, probably a handkerchief, that appeared to have been rolled and pushed into the body, most probably up the rectum, or possibly into the lower portion of the vagina. No reason or explanation for this peculiar circumstance was ever advanced.

The Times of 13 June reported that the body was accompanied by 'an old brown linsey dress, red selvedge, two flounces round the bottom, waistband made of small blue-and-white check material like duster cloth, a piece of canvas roughly sewn on the end of the band, a large brass pin in the skirt and a black dress button, about the size of a threepenny piece, with lines across in the pocket'.

The torn pieces of ulster coat in which some of the pieces had been wrapped was grey with a black cross-hatching pattern forming a check design. The material was of good quality, but old. Old, too, were the pair of women's drawers bearing the name L. E. Fisher.

The police view was that it was extremely unlikely that the deceased's name was L. E. Fisher. There was, however, a Hertfordshire policeman, Constable Fisher, who had a twenty-five-year-old sister who was missing. Although her official cognomen was Mrs Wren, her maiden name had indeed been L. E. Fisher. She had abandoned her husband and child in May 1888 to live with another man. Whether she was the same L. E. Fisher as the barmaid Laura E. Fisher, working at the Old Cock Tavern in Highbury, who was subsequently found alive and well and living in Ramsgate, is not a matter of record.

By the time of the opening of the inquest on 15 June, the police had been carrying out extensive searches for the dead woman's missing head. They made use of dogs, Waring's Smoker among them. Nothing was found. Inquests were held on bodies in the areas where they were discovered, and since most of the body parts had been found on the south bank of the river, the jurisdiction fell to the mid-Surrey coroner, Athelstan Braxton Hicks. He presided over the inquiry opened in the Star and Garter, in Battersea, on 16 June. Dr Bond was the first witness. Thereafter, assured by Inspector Tunbridge that enquiries were still ongoing, Braxton Hicks adjourned the inquest until 1 July.

Then, very suddenly, a breakthrough.

A Mrs Catharine Jackson came forward to identify the

dead woman *not* as L. E. Fisher but as her own daughter, Elizabeth. The corpse lying in Battersea Mortuary was in a pretty advanced state of decomposition, but Mrs Jackson recognised it as being that of her daughter by the small scar on her left forearm, caused by an accident with a vase when she was about twelve. The scar was revealed on the decomposing arm by lifting a piece of skin and exposing the scar tissue.

Elizabeth had been twenty-four years old, five feet and five inches tall, plump and well formed. She had bright reddish-gold hair, good teeth and nicely shaped hands, but her nails were bitten to the quick. The ulster had been given to her by a family friend, Mary Minter, not long before she disappeared. And the police discovered that Elizabeth had bought old clothes labelled L. E. Fisher in Ipswich. She was the youngest of three daughters – the others were Annie and May – born to Mr John Jackson, a stonemason, and his wife, Catharine, in Chelsea, in 1865. In 1881, when she was sixteen, she had gone out to work as a domestic servant in the neighbourhood of Chelsea. She had been described as 'of excellent character' until, in November 1888, something happened which occasioned her leaving both her job and her home. Thereafter, she had been living in various common lodging houses in the vicinity of Chelsea. Her last known address was 14 Turk's Row, which was near Chelsea Barracks.

Strangely, Elizabeth's father, in a letter to one of his other daughters, had written of his fear that the Thames victim might have been the missing Elizabeth. The last member of her family to see her around that time was her sister Annie. She met her in the street, in Turk's Row, just off Sloane Square. The girls had a nasty row, Annie accusing Elizabeth of picking up men for immoral purposes. The accusation was well founded. She was living with a 'protector', *aliter* as a prostitute.

In the November of 1888, by which time she was well

known to the local police, she took up with a casually met Cambridgeshire man, a thirty-seven-year-old millstone grinder named John Fairclough, with whom she moved to Ipswich, in January 1889. The pair were in Colchester on 30 March 1889, and, unable to find work there, walked all the way back to London, where they settled into lodgings in Manilla Street, Millwall, taking a room at four shillings a week, with a Mrs Kate Paine, who would afterwards testify that Fairclough was violent in his treatment of Elizabeth, knocking her about, irrespective of her being five months pregnant.

The pair parted on 28 April, Fairclough going off to Croydon in search of a job. He was subsequently traced to Tipton St John, in Devonshire. He expressed his willingness to co-operate with the police. He said that he was thirty-six years old, born in March 1853, in Cambridgeshire, and a millstone dresser by trade. He had first met Elizabeth Jackson in a public house on the corner of Turk's Row. She had told him that she had been living with a man named Charlie. The relationship was over. Fairclough had invited her to accompany him to Ipswich, where he had obtained a few months' work, and she had agreed to do so. He had wanted her to go with him to Croydon, but she refused, saying that she wanted to stay with her mother until her baby was born. This would have been difficult, as her mother was at that time lodged in the workhouse.

As a matter of fact, Mrs Jackson did see her daughter once more. It was on 31 May 1889, only a day or two before she was murdered. The encounter took place in Queen's Road, Chelsea. Elizabeth's initial reaction upon seeing her mother was to be poised for flight, but, relenting, she stayed put, and the two spent time together, Elizabeth reciting to her mother the long litany of her woes.

After separating from Fairclough, Elizabeth was doubtless driven to resume her old habits, solicitously promenading near Battersea Bridge and the Albert Palace, plying her trade, along with a number of other young women at that time, actually in Battersea Park, it being her boast that she had been in the habit of remaining in there after the park gates had been closed. For a time she was reduced to sleeping *al fresco*, rough on the benches on Chelsea Embankment.

There was a contemporary tendency to link the later Thames murders with Jack the Ripper. It has been said that there was absolutely no justification for this; it was just another expression of the overwhelming obsession with Saucy Jacky that held the population in its stranglehold. Nevertheless, that the killings and mutilations of '87, '88 and '89 were the work of one pair of hands, a single killer, does seem possible, even extremely likely.

Part Three
The Commission of a Murder

Death on a Summer's Evening

The year 1910 stood between the gentle demise of the great Victorian epoch and the genteel expiry of the Edwardian afternoon. The king had died in May. A fifth George sat upon the throne of an England which, within less than a half-decade, was to alter out of all recognition.

16 July 1910. A Saturday. 9.30 p.m. A beautiful summer's evening. A red-sunlight-trimmed twilight is creeping westward up the river and over the barely stirring trees to shroud Battersea Park. Deep in the surrounding red-brick mansion belt of Battersea stands a nominally bilocational building. It is primarily identified as No. 17 Prince of Wales Road, but its secondary title is No. 8 Clifton Gardens, which latter is a short terrace forming a portion of the early part of Prince of Wales Road.

This binomial house, tall, prim, red-flushed, rises three storeys high at the corner of Prince of Wales and Rosenau roads. Each of its three floors is a separate purpose-built flat. In July 1910, that on the ground floor (8A) was empty, had been for some eight months and was then undergoing restoration, repair and redecoration. The third floor, top (8C), was in the tenancy of a man named Samuel Butcher. He and the family dog were away that weekend. The middle, second-floor flat (8B) was occupied by a Miss Elizabeth Earle.

Suddenly, the sharp, reverberating reports of two rapidly successive pistol shots shattered and scattered the evening's sweet peace.

Edward Noice, a taxicab driver, is walking along Rosenau Road, where he lives at No. 45. He is startled by the noise, and even more startled to see, on the far side of the garden wall that surrounds Cambridge House, the girls' school next-door to 17 Prince of Wales Road, a man breaking through the Cambridge House garden trees. As he watches, the man clambers up on to the top of the wall, rolls over as quickly as he can, drops into Rosenau Road, turns left, and pelts up into Petworth Street, up Albert Bridge Road, and away as fast as his legs will carry him in the direction of the Albert Bridge, and the river.

Noice contacts Harold Glanville, his neighbour, at No. 41, and tells him what he has seen. They both drive straight and speedily round to Battersea Police Station, in nearby Battersea Bridge Road. There Noice sees the duty officer, Sergeant Willie Buckley, and tells him that he thought the shots had seemed to have come from the rear of No. 17 Prince of Wales Road, and how he saw the man running away from Cambridge House. Buckley decides that he ought to go and investigate. Noice straightaway drives him round there.

Part Four
An Actor's Background

2

The Family Way

Thomas Anderson, a farmer's son, was born in Liverpool on 6 August 1820. He was baptised there, at St Peter's, Church Street, in 1826. On 20 September 1849, at Prittlewell in Essex, he married Louisa Sutherland. She, born in Scotland in 1823 or 1824, was the daughter of a shoemaker. Since both Thomas and Louisa gave Prittlewell Priory as their residence at the time of their marriage, and since one of the witnesses at their wedding, Elizabeth Eades, was the cook at the Priory, and Thomas was a coachman, it seems likely that he was in the employ of Daniel Robert Scratton, justice of the peace and master of Prittlewell Priory, and that Louisa was also working for that powerful family, perhaps as a maidservant. The Andersons' other witness, Charles Brett, is described on the census form as a gardener. He does not live at the Priory, but it is very probable that he worked there.

Thomas and Louisa's first child, daughter Louisa, was born to them in Liverpool in 1851. About that time Thomas was employed as a coachman in domestic service. He and his wife were by then living at the Grove Lodge, at Ditton, just south of the village of Cronton, then in the borough of Widnes, and situated some twelve miles south-east of Liverpool.

No time wasted, a second daughter, Mary Jane, arrived in 1852. The Andersons were then still quartered in Ditton.

Their third daughter, Emma, came along in 1854, following the family's move to Victoria Buildings, Victoria Road, Aigburth, an old-fashioned, green suburb situated to the south of Liverpool's Sefton Park, bounded on the east by the River Mersey and the district known locally as 'The Holy Land', where the astronomer Jeremiah Horrocks (born: Toxteth, 1618; died: Toxteth, 1641), first observer of the transit of Venus, dwelt. Go a little further south and you come to Riversdale Road. There stands Battlecrease House, where James Maybrick died, allegedly murdered by his wife, Florence, with arsenic, in 1889. Fecund territory.

The Andersons' fourth girl-child, Caroline, put in her appearance at Aigburth in 1857, where she was followed, in 1859, by Edith. Harriet, the Andersons' sixth and final daughter, was also Aigburth-born, in 1861.

It was not long after the family's removal from Aigburth to Much Woolton, a village five miles to the south-east of Liverpool, that the couple's seventh and last child, a son, christened Thomas Weldon, after his uncle Thomas Lightfoot Weldon, first saw the light of day on 23 December 1861 at a small house in Woolton Street. On the new baby's birth certificate, the father's occupation is shown as that of carriage proprietor.

A decade later the family was dispersed. Thomas and Louisa, together with their daughters Edith and Harriet, had deserted their last Much Woolton address – No. 8 Acrefield Road. Daughter Louisa was away in Liverpool, one of a number of drapers' assistants lodging at 13–15 Church Street. Jane, also working in Liverpool, was living at 26–28 St Peter's Lane. Thomas Weldon, aged nine, and his fifteen-year-old sister, Emma, were living with their uncle, Thomas Lightfoot Weldon, and aunt, Jane Gordon Weldon, at 11 Tufnell Park Road, London.

Uncle Tom Weldon (1829–1913) was London born – Burton Street, W.C.1 – and bred, baptised at St George's, Hanover Square. In December 1853, describing himself as a stationer, he married Jane Gordon Sutherland, a Scotswoman born in Banffshire around 1824–6. Her father, John Sutherland, was a bootmaker. It is likely that she was the sister of Anderson's wife Louisa.

Thomas Weldon originally earned his living as a commercial traveller, or bagman as they were called in those days, but he seems also to have been a pretty astute dealer in commercial properties of various kinds, taking part in the sale of land, buildings and businesses.

On 19 November 1881, he was advertising in the *Reading Mercury* the disposal by private treaty of freehold land and buildings, 'all that valuable plot of land with tenements thereon, situate in Bridge Street, Maidenhead'.

In the *Leicester Chronicle* of 4 March 1882, he was seeking to effect the immediate disposal of a printing, stationery and bookselling business 'in an increasing town in one of the Midland counties. The oldest established business, and occupying the best situation in the town.'

In October 1884, he was advertising in the *London Standard*: 'To Booksellers, Stationers, and Printers – partner wanted, in a fine old business, established 50 years, in a thriving country town: Conservative preferred; about 1200*l* required.'

He was advertising in the *Reading Mercury* of 4 August 1888: 'Provincial Press. An excellent printing and stationery business, together with old-established county newspaper for disposal. Proprietor retiring. Applicants must have £4,000 at command.'

14 April 1890. *London Daily News*. 'Partner wanted to join advertiser in opening a printing business. A practical man required. Capital about £1,000. In large suburb near London. In present hands in the stationery over 30 years. Printing connection already established.'

6 October 1891. *London Daily News.* 'CHEMISTS.
– For Disposal, in consequence decease of proprietor, an
old-established concern in Guernsey. Several specialities.
About £300 for stock, fixtures, and fittings, very cheap.'

And in the same issue: 'Printing and stationery business
for disposal in Devonshire. Will bear every investigation.
Old established. Good connection. All at a valuation,
about £800. – Apply to Mr T. L. Weldon. 62 Tufnell
Park Road, London, N.'

That Weldon was a man of determined character
is nicely illustrated by an incident reported in the
Leicester Journal of 25 April 1879. Alfred Leeming,
who stated that he was a commission agent and resided
at Manchester, was charged with stealing an overcoat, a
pocketbook, a pair of gloves, a tobacco pouch, a Turkish
cap and a neckerchief, value £3 10s, the property of
Thomas Lightfoot Weldon, at Ashby-de-la-Zouch. The
prosecutor was a commercial traveller who had been
staying at the Queen's Head Hotel. On the morning of
16 April he went out on business, leaving his overcoat
hanging in the commercial room, with all the various
objects mentioned in its pockets. On returning to the
hotel he found that his coat had gone. He informed
the police and then caught the one o'clock train to
his next business port of call, Burton. On reaching
Grealey, where the train stopped, he saw the thief on
the platform there with the stolen coat on his arm. The
man got on to the train. Weldon at once left the carriage
in which he was seated, went into that which the thief
had entered, and, on arriving at Burton, gave him into
the custody of the police. In answer to the magistrate's
question as to whether anything was known against the
prisoner, Weldon supplied a comprehensive history of
his malfeasances at different hotels during the last few
months. The prisoner admitted a previous conviction as
a rogue and vagabond, and was sentenced to six weeks'
hard labour.

Weldon survived his namesake nephew by three years, dying on 3 December 1913. He had lost his wife in 1893. She died at 62 Tufnell Park Road. He left a legacy of £416 12s 11d to his niece Annie Price, who had been living with him since 1881 and must, in his latter years, have acted as his companion, or, as we would call it nowadays, his carer.

Time had begun to ring its distressful changes on the Andersons. About the year 1873, Thomas Anderson *père* died. On a more cheerful note, it seems likely that sister Emma married in 1876, in Whitechapel. Her husband's name was Alfred Beard. They had a child, Margaret, around 1882. Emma was widowed by 1901.

By 1881, the widowed Louisa Anderson and her chicks, Caroline, Edith and Thomas, were all snugly settled into No. 4 Cornwall Villas, Yerbury Road, Upper Holloway, just round the corner from Uncle Tom Lightfoot's.

Nineteen-year-old Thomas was less snugly settled into his daily job; he was, somewhat disgruntledly, working in the lace trade. Sister Louisa was living and working in Sheffield, as a mantle cutter-out, and lodging at Ecclesall Bierlow. Sister Mary Jane had a job as a milliner at a ladies' outfitters at No. 2 Station Parade, Sydenham Road, Sydenham. Sister Harriet was working as a general servant for a father and son at No. 36 Derby Road, North Meols, in the vicinity of Southport.

On 8 June 1893, aged sixty-eight years, Louisa Anderson died in London.

It was around this time that Thomas Weldon Anderson was just starting out on his career behind the footlights.

3

A Strolling Player, He

Foursquare on the perch of his early teens, having acquired the necessary erudition of the three Rs, Thomas Weldon Anderson entered the wage-earning world in London as a clerk in the lace trade. Such a situation was not to his taste, and he turned a wistfully ambitious eye to the more seductive prospect of the stage. By hook and by crook, he somehow succeeded in planting a foot on the elusive boards.

This was the heyday of the theatre; in the pre-wireless era, when the cinema and television were unheard of, the theatre and the music hall were the chief sources of public entertainment. And they were big business. Every city, every town, had its theatre; more often than not several. Plays, playlets and sketches were voraciously consumed, and there was a healthy demand for actors and actresses.

But there was a snag. It was considered perverse even to think of becoming an actor or actress. All too often travelling Thespians found themselves undeservedly despised and derided; the 'welcome' mat swept from beneath their feet, the door slammed in their faces. 'We don't want your sort here.' Actors, stage folk, were unquestionably beyond the pale, anathema to people who regarded themselves as respectable.

A newspaper article of 1882, 'Wanderers on the Face of the Earth', neatly encompassed the orbit of current popular calumnies:

> Actors are usually those of weak intellect, who readily enter a profession with no appeal to their more intelligent brethren. Although fully aware of their limitations, they cling on doggedly to a sinking ship. Theirs is the waste of a life without the saving grace of aspiration. Let them into our home? Never! The social habits of the dissipated and shiftless majority which make up the ranks of touring companies indicate that they are quite happy to pursue their own road to hell.

Turn to the stage and one was voluntarily joining the legion of the lost – mountebanks, rogues and vagabonds. That is, of course, unless one ascended the rarefied heights to become a Henry Irving, Herbert Beerbohm Tree or George Alexander – an actor-manager theatrical knight.

Although superficially it may have seemed romantic and attractive – the lure of the lights, the call boy's shout, the enrapturing thunder of applause – the life of the itinerant jobbing actor was no picnic. Beyond the deceptive dazzle of the footlights it was compounded of disillusion and discomfort. And be under no delusion, it was a hard school, demanding the ability and the willingness to cope with a bewildering variety of successive parts, low comedy and high tragedy, on alternate nights; to manufacture laughter and tears on demand. There was, moreover, no route by which a destination of success could be arrived at, save by virtue of rigid, unfaltering dedication to a harsh, exhausting and sometimes health-sacrificing apprenticeship, accompanied by the attendance of a generous measure of luck.

The front-of-house mystery and charm was a carefully wrought, painstakingly architected creation, which, unless lovingly nurtured, would evaporate swift as the pantomimic genie escaped the bottle. Its beguiling essence was assuredly lacking as you, apprentice initiate of the mimetic art, picking your cautious way along a dingy, draughty, ill-lit, backstage corridor, encounter disturbing shadows that lurk and flicker in the dark and dusty underworld below the stage, or come face to face with the aura of spent despair that hovers above the cluster of drained beer bottles forlorn upon the dressing-room side table. It is now that the romance tends to fade from the theatrical firmament.

Neither was the time-honoured custom of 'travelling on one's luggage' to the town of one's next engagement precisely conducive to contentment. The endless Sunday train journeys, ungraciously punctuated by interminable waits on the platform at Crewe. The next port of theatrical call might turn out to be a discouragingly damp and decaying structure situated hard by a stagnant stretch of canal, tattered posters of long-forgotten presentations fluttering dejectedly in the blusters of a nagging wind.

It was, moreover, far from unknown for a train to arrive at a new town and disgorge its sleep-bleared Thespian cargo at six or seven in the morning. Then it would be a rapid scamper round to the digs – always provided that digs had been sagaciously booked in advance – to swallow a snatched breakfast before rushing to the theatre to pick up letters and telegrams, and give necessary attentions to items of costume. After a rest in the afternoon, there would likely be only a light meal served before the evening performance.

On other occasions it could be after midnight when the company steamed into town. The local residents would by then be well tucked up for the night, curtains drawn, windows dark, front doors locked and sealed. Frankly uninviting. The actors and actresses, cold and depressed, would set forth on the long tramp quartering the dead streets for food and lodging. When all else failed they would be driven to knocking up the caretaker of the theatre or hall where they were booked to appear, and once let in they would gratefully bed down in the least uninviting corners for a few hours' sleep. Next day the search would resume for the room that would be 'home' for the succeeding seven nights. Always waiting in the wings was the disappointment of arrival at unwelcoming cold-comfort digs, where unappetising food was grudgingly served by a grim-faced, life-soured harridan masquerading as a jolly theatrical 'Ma'.

It wasn't, of course, always like that. There were divine, shining exceptions; saintly theatrical Mas who looked after the dejected players that life threw upon their lodgings' doorsteps as solicitously as if they were their own blood kin. Piping hot-water bottles. Never a damp sheet. Bacon-and-egg breakfasts, with occasional additional garnish of sausage, tomato and mushrooms. A plenitude of cups of strong, mahogany-brown tea. And so to bed and a good sleep, with a satisfying supper's full stomach.

Such gratuitous luxury must needs be thrown into the balance against premises offering sundry sanitary hazards. There were reports from such middle-sized towns as Rawtenstall and Rotherham, Fleetwood and Stockton, of damp beds, insufficient bedclothes and infestations of fleas, bedbugs, rats and mice. You could, it was said, smell the bedbugs, and a visual giveaway to be watched out for was the strategic placement of hopeful cups of disinfectant under the bedposts.

In *'Neath the Mask*, John M. East's enthralling account of the East family and its distinguished place in the theatrical history of London, he writes,

In the West Country digs were easier to find. In fact, at one or two halts in Devon and Somerset landladies would actually queue up outside the station as the 'pro train' pulled in, and barter on the spot for terms.

Accommodation rarely cost more than twelve shillings a week with full board, which consisted of three good meals a day, and a place in the sitting-room beside a roaring fire during the hours of leisure. In the bigger towns the older men and women in the cast recommend their regular 'Ma's', who attended to their every need for nominal reward.

Each Monday brought the challenge of a new and hopefully sympathetically receptive audience. One came to recognise that the reaction of audiences to the same play differed, sometimes quite substantially, from town to town. The Princess's at Glasgow, for instance, could be – and often was – a distinctly rowdy venue. So was the Govan Lyceum. Audiences who patronised the Royal at Brighton were sophisticated and well ordered. The retired gentry who kept the Cheltenham Opera House prosperously busy were notably well mannered and appreciative.

For their part the peripatetic actors had to remember to pitch their voices adequately for the area in which they happened to be performing. Sheffield, for example, a town where ears were dimmed by perpetual steely noise and clatter, demanded a necessarily higher pitch than a gentler seafaring town such as Plymouth, where it was permissible to speak more gently and intimately.

It had perhaps been Uncle Tom Weldon, pressing into beneficial service the influence of his long years as a bagman in the cloth industry, who secured for his nephew a sound and respectable clerkship in the London office of a lace firm, and it calls for no great feat of imagination to appreciate his feelings at seeing, after all the plotting and scheming and effort which he had put in to tuck his nephew into a nice, cosy berth in the elegant lace trade, the lad throw it all away and enter the disreputable world of the theatre.

As it was, young Anderson had gone, in accordance

with Uncle Weldon's cherished plan, straight from school to a proscribed life on a high stool, where, hour upon unforgiving hour, emblematic figures of commerce danced meaninglessly before him between the columns of the ledgers, like the gyrations of the fortification spectra of migraine. Throughout the long tedium of endless-seeming days he would yearn away the hours until eventide, when the shutters came down at the office and he could make off to some beloved theatre to see the curtain come up. And all the while the urge to act was quickening in his blood. As to precisely when – or how – he effected his escape from the desk's dead wood to the living boards of the stage is not a matter of record, but for the next forty years it would be his embraced destiny to criss-cross Britain treading the boards of hundreds of theatres.

4
Curtain Calls
1884–1899

It was at his hometown Liverpool's Rotunda Theatre that twenty-four-year-old Thomas Weldon Anderson, theatrically transmogrified by the flickering magic of the footlights into Weldon Atherstone, actor, made his appearance on the Monday of the week commencing 29 March 1886, in a six-night special production by Mr Stafford Grafton's High-Class London Company of Tom Taylor's *The Ticket-of-Leave Man*, the part he played being that of 'Tiger' Dalton, whom, opined the critics, he 'satisfactorily depicted'.

Stafford Grafton was in fact something of a newcomer; a very young, up-and-coming actor – he had just attained his majority – who, with his wife, had recently established a London company. He was said to exhibit 'not only a taste for his calling, but high abilities for the impersonations of extremely difficult parts'. He had a mellow voice, graceful figure and a winning command in his renderings. Although he had only been before the public for a short time, he could take the parts of Hawkshaw in *The Ticket-of-Leave Man* and Raphael de Correze in *Moths* with such vigour and style as would compare well with the performances of some who had spent almost a lifetime on the stage. It was predicted that he might be expected to rank among some of the foremost in his profession.

By that March Monday, Atherstone (as we must now call him) had a fair bit of acting experience under his belt, as witness a notice inserted by him in the theatrical paper *The Stage* of Friday 13 February 1885, in which he announces that, having concluded on 7 February a stock season of eleven weeks at the Theatre Royal, Inverness, he is now 'at liberty', inviting offers for 'Juveniles, Light Comedy, and Gentlemanly Heavies, &c.', and supplying the permanent address 62 Tufnell Park Road, Holloway, London, N. Clearly, he has been working in the theatre since at least November 1884, and most likely before that.

In the 27 February 1885 issue of *The Stage*, Mr Weldon Atherstone thanks T. Sennett, Esq. and R. Liston, Esq. for offers, but remains 'at liberty'. He continues 'liberated' in *The Stage* issues of 6 March and 13 March 1885.

In the last weeks of 1885, a twenty-year-old Irishwoman by the name of Monica Kelly was just coming to the end of a two-year contract, touring throughout Ireland with the popular Irish comedian Charles Cooke. According to Jonathan Goodman's *Acts of Murder*, we know the following about Monica. The daughter of a law clerk, she had in fact been pursuing a theatrical career for some time, as borne out by her entries in *The Stage* of 15 and 29 January 1886, intimating her readiness to undertake 'Irish Parts, Singing and Walking Ladies'. In the January of 1886, she had taken a boat from Dublin, where she lived at 45 Irishtown Road, across the Irish Sea to Liverpool, and found theatrical lodgings at 15 Greek Street. These lodgings, kept by publican John Sinclair and his wife, Minnie, were reasonable – '12s Bedroom and Sitting Room. Piano. Clean, comfortable. Highest references. Near theatres.' It was here that she made a first passing acquaintance with Weldon Atherstone.

For him the year 1886 had begun sufficiently low-key and humble, with an announcement in *The Stage* of 15 January advertising him as 'Disengaged', otherwise 'At Liberty' or 'Resting', *vulgo*: out of work. He is braced to play 'Juveniles, Aristocratic Heavies, &c'. This time the address he gives is 15 Greek Street, Liverpool. He does not repine long. Readers of *The Stage* learned from a triumphant insertion in the issue of 19 February 1886 that January's bait has been taken. This communication emanates from the Winter Gardens, Blackpool, where Atherstone has obviously landed an engagement, and whither he has been accompanied by Monica, who remains there with him from 5 to 18 February, when she returns to Dublin.

Meanwhile, Atherstone has been engaged by Stafford Grafton, Esq. to tour with his company and a repertoire of Ouida's *Moths*, Tom Taylor's *The Ticket-of-Leave Man*, Lord Lytton's *The Lady of Lyons* and the musical farce *Perfection*, and is performing in them from 15 to 20 March at the Theatre Royal, Barnsley, and from 21 to 26 March at the Theatre Royal, West Bromwich.

Monica is appearing with Atherstone at Jarrow on 28 May 1886, playing the Duchess de Sonnage in *Moths*. The following week they are at the Theatre Royal, West Hartlepool, for six nights, when he proudly inserts in *The Stage* of 4 June 1886 the intelligence that he has been specially engaged by Mr Stafford Grafton for the part of Correze in *Moths*. Throughout the week of 14–19 June 1886, the pair were at the Theatre Royal, South Shields.

During the August of 1886, Atherstone was acting under the company banner of Messrs J. K. Murray and Wilton Reed. The play in which he was appearing at the Theatre Royal, Wigan, entitled *Driven from Home*, franked by the typical sentimental bravura displayed by so many of the plays which the multitude of theatres required and so avidly consumed, was described as 'a pathetic and realistic drama'.

The outcast in the play was Laura Raybrooke, daughter of a rich man of greedy and ill-tempered turn of mind, and upon her marrying a poor, though honest, young man, he thrusts her from his house and forbids her to return. Driven from home, she and her husband live for a year in abject poverty, at the end of which time the husband is shot dead. Thrown, unprotected, on the world with her young child, the widow seeks the shelter of her father's home, only to be turned away once more. The person who is so influencing her father against her is her cousin, Geoffrey Waring, who had at one time wanted to marry her – merely, it must be said, so that he might thus inherit his uncle's fortune. But now, seeing his plans frustrated, he wants to have her and her child put out of the way, so that he may become the only rightful heir. Ultimately, Laura falls in the snow and perishes. Her orphaned child is well cared for by her faithful servants, and after a lapse of a few years he is apprenticed in a sawmill, where a dastardly attempt to murder him, at the instigation of Geoffrey Waring, is happily frustrated. The piece ends with the restoration of the boy to his grandfather, who has long sought for him, and the arrest of Geoffrey Waring and his confederates.

Atherstone took the part of the villainous Waring and did it proud, earning much praise.

In the November of 1886 (between the 1st and the 6th), at the Royal Alhambra Theatre, Barrow-in-Furness, Atherstone was personating, with critically acclaimed distinction, the unscrupulous Oswald Brandon in J. K. Murray's rewritten version of A. Melville's *Not Guilty*. From 31 January to 5 February 1887, Messrs Murray & Reed were presenting *Perfection* at the Theatre Royal, Rotherham, together with *Millions of Money*, with Blanche pleasingly played by Monica Kelly and Weldon Atherstone punching in with his customary excellence as the Marquis. The following week (7–12 February) *Driven from Home* was the bill at Wakefield's Theatre

Royal, and on Wednesday (9th) and Friday (11th) Atherstone was appearing in *Not Guilty*.

Weldon and Monica were acting together in *Driven from Home* at Macdermott's Star Theatre, Wolverhampton, during the weeks of 27 June–8 July 1887. His interpretation of the evil Waring was hailed as cool and calculating, 'though it is a pity he pitches his voice in such a sepulchral key'. Monica was picked out for special mention.

Despite a notice in *The Stage* of 8 July 1887 of his resignation from his arrangement with Messrs Murray & Reed, and the announcement of his availability for 'Juvenile Lead and Gentlemanly Heavies', we find Mr Weldon Atherstone appearing at the Theatre Royal, Macclesfield, in *Driven from Home* from 21 to 26 November 1887. In January 1888, Atherstone, 'a clever actor, plays well as Ernest Saville' in *Not Guilty* at the Royal Alhambra Theatre, Barrow-in-Furness, and 'Miss Monica Kelly as Nan scores heavily'.

The pair are back at Barrow-in-Furness the following July, together again, in *Next-of-Kin*, Weldon Atherstone as Hugh Ayrton and Monica Kelly, who is 'quite a character', as Jenny. And during the week immediately preceding the terrifying eruption in East End London of the homicidal monster Jack the Ripper, 27 August–1 September 1888, Atherstone was at the Queen's Royal Theatre, Dublin, in Boucicault's *Arrah-na-Pogue*, in which he 'made a capital Major Coffin'.

Thomas Weldon Atherstone and Monica Kelly married at Salford, Manchester, in the autumn of 1888, both giving their address as 20 Barlows Road, Salford, and their occupation as 'comedians'. Born in Ireland in 1865, the bride was four years younger than the groom, and already *enceinte*.

Christmas Eve 1888 found Atherstone in the part of George Palmer in *Simple Hearts*, a domestic drama in six acts by C. H. Lorenzo, which was being played for the first time in the Public Hall at Wrexham. Act One opens in the woods at Elmsleigh, the house of the hero and heroine, Frank Fairleigh and Ruth Allen; and we learn that Frank is secretly married to Ruth, who is a simple country maiden, the daughter of a poor farmer. Frank has just received orders to join his regiment in Africa for the war. Not knowing of the marriage, George Palmer, a young gamekeeper upon the estate who has been in love with Ruth since childhood, meets Frank and questions him as to his intentions. Frank promises to make Ruth his wife on his return, and Palmer is satisfied. They part good friends, Frank leaving Ruth in Palmer's charge. Some scenes, vividly depicting the popularity of Frank in the village, follow, and we then find ourselves in Fairleigh House, where Admiral Fairleigh declares his intention of leaving his property in such a manner that, unless Frank marries his cousin Florence, the whole will go to an old servant, Ben Rakins, who has sailed with him for over forty years. Florence, who is engaged to Gerald Kingsley, decides to give him up in favour of the fortune; but when Kingsley suggests a plan by which she can marry him and get the property as well, they arrange to get Ruth away. Florence compels Simon Grigg, a country postman, to detain certain letters, and substitute one that is supposed to have come from Frank, telling Ruth that he cannot see her again. This has the desired effect of making Ruth think Frank faithless, and the act closes with the arrest of George Palmer for a supposed attempt to rob Fairleigh House, the result of a plot carried into execution by two tramps who have been in the village.

The next act shows us Palmer's return after three months in prison, when he finds his old parents dead and Ruth gone away. He again vows to find Frank and see Ruth righted, and in the next scene meets Ruth in lodgings in London, where she is being persecuted by Gerald Kingsley, who, having discovered that she was really married to Frank, now offers to marry her himself, as she has been led to believe that her husband has been killed abroad. Palmer arrives just as she is almost dying of starvation and to save her commits highway robbery, his victim being Gerald Kingsley, who, finding some of his property in Ruth's house, threatens to give her in charge if she does not consent to marry him. To save her, George confesses his crime, and they are both arrested. Thus ends the second act.

The third opens in Africa, where Frank and George Palmer meet. Frank confesses that he is married to Ruth, and hears that she is dead, Palmer having been told that she died of brain fever in the hospital. The act closes with an attempt upon Frank's life by a Zulu warrior, who is shot by Palmer. After this we again find ourselves at Elmsleigh. Frank is expected home, and after some lively comedy scenes the admiral imparts to Frank his views as to the latter's marriage with Florence, to which he (Frank) finally reluctantly consents, and the marriage is arranged to the satisfaction of Gerald and his colleague.

This may be the juncture at which to mention the mystery of Constance Caroline Anderson. She appears, aged three, in the 1891 census (April), and is described as the niece of Edith and Harriet Anderson, with whom she is then living at 80 Mercers Road, Upper Holloway. She is said to have been born at Darwen, in Lancashire, presumably in 1888. She was undoubtedly Atherstone and Monica's prenuptially conceived offspring. They married before her birth, but, finding it impossible to cope with the baby during their rigorous theatrical travels, they had 'deposited' her in the willing care of Harriet Anderson, with whom she was to remain for the rest of her life.

Their first 'official' marital offspring was their son, Thomas Frederick, born on 30 December 1889, at Kirkdale, Liverpool. Their third child was a daughter, Doris Monica, born in 1891 in Manchester.

By the time of the next census, 1901, Constance, now

thirteen, is still living at Mercers Road with Edith and Harriet.

The 1921 census shows her as Constance Caroline Anderson, a spinster aged thirty-one, living with her aunts Harriet, Louisa and Caroline Anderson at 62 Tufnell Park Road, Holloway. She is described as a 'shorthand typist, commercial', and working as a doctor's secretary. She died at 62 Tufnell Park Road on 18 March 1921, aged thirty-one years, of rectal carcinoma, with secondary growths in the liver and peritoneum. Her death, certified by Dr F. de Boissierè, MRCS, was registered by her aunt Harriet.

Weldon and Monica were sharing the stage again in August 1889, this time at the St James's Theatre, Manchester. The vehicle was a drama in five acts, *False Evidence*.

Plot: An Irish gentleman, one Dennis O'Neal, has two children, Connor and Nelly. The son has imbibed strong Home Rule prejudices from his association with the peasantry and tenant farmers with whom he has been constantly associated from childhood. In consequence of this and various machinations of the steward, Michael McCarthy, he is disinherited and cast adrift. Dennis O'Neal becomes enamoured of Judith, who is the discarded mistress of the villainous, McCarthy, whose son is thus favoured in his pretensions to become the old man's heir. In the first act we find Connor O'Neal protecting his sister from her supposed cousin, Walter Delaney, an illegitimate son of Mrs O'Neal. Pat Molloy, the village scapegrace, got, by an artifice, a hundred pounds from McCarthy, who is dunning the needy squire for debts, in order to assist his son and mistress, and prevent the restoration of the rightful heir to the affections of his father. Pat Molloy pays the debt to the steward with his own money, and thus for a time staves off the imprisonment and ruin of the family, and enables the squire to return to his regiment.

In the second act Dennis O'Neal returns, repeating his harshness to his son, and saves the little estate from the clutches of the conspirators by revoking his former will and making another. In the struggle which ensues Delaney enters, picks up a knife which has been dropped, and in a frenzy at the return of Dennis O'Neal plunges the weapon by mistake into the heart of McCarthy, and charges Dennis with the murder, sundry circumstances giving a probable appearance to the justice of the charge.

In the third act we find Delaney married to Nelly, Connor's sister, who has become his wife upon the understanding that her father is not charged with the capital crime. Dennis is condemned upon the minor charge of manslaughter, and is sentenced to a long period of penal servitude. Delaney now tires of Nelly, and disavows the legality of their marriage, the chapel of St Bridget's having been burnt down almost immediately after the ceremony. But Pat Molloy, ever alert in the interest of his friends, has secured the parish register from the smoking ruins, and temporarily hidden it in the smithy of Philip McGrath, who is Nelly's former lover. Dennis O'Neal, favoured by the warders, escapes from Galway Gaol, and, by a change of costume with Pat Molloy, manages to avoid his pursuers. But the orders being to take O'Neal dead or alive, Delaney contrives to shoot him. The old man, dying, leaves a legacy of vengeance to his son.

In the last two acts, principally by the efforts of Pat Molloy, the disinherited son returns. Delaney, who is about to become a bigamist in order to procure a large fortune, is intercepted in his designs by Molloy, who gives the register of the old chapel to the priest, and by so doing saves the heiress, Lady Helen Fermoy. Delaney, baffled, sets fire to the priest's house, where Nelly is living. She is rescued by her brother, Connor, who, meeting Delaney, engages with him in a struggle in the course of which Delaney is accidentally shot by

Tim O'Toole, his rascally bailiff. Nelly is united to Philip McGrath, and all ends happily.

Atherstone, as Walter Delaney, made an excellent villain, and Monica, as Molly Malony, carried away a large share of honour.

In *Jane Shore*, playing in September 1889 at the Public Hall, Bacup, the story is told of how the crafty Richard, Duke of Gloucester, accomplishes his object of setting aside the title of Queen Elizabeth Woodville to the throne in succession to King Edward IV, becoming the reigning monarch himself through the terrible means of murdering the late king's two young sons in the Tower of London. In this play, Atherstone scored what was perhaps the greatest hit of his entire career. His performance was being talked of with the bated breath of unrestricted admiration twenty years later. Monica played beside him, the part of Alison Yeast.

Throughout the last decade of the nineteenth century Weldon Atherstone prospered moderately. His acting was admired, consistently praised in critiques. He remained in fairly constant demand, and was seldom enforcedly resting for long.

He opened his second decade on the stage by announcing in *The Era* of 22 March 1890 that 'Mr Weldon Atherstone has arranged with Mr J. F. Preston to undertake the Management of his "Jane Shore" Company B.' Between March and July, he duly presented it at Newport, Consett, Skipton and the Theatre Royal, Birkenhead. Thereafter, he filled very efficiently the part of Amos Knight in J. Hewetson-Porter's *Victory*, at the Gaiety Theatre and Opera House, Burnley, and the Queen's Theatre, Birmingham.

The Hand of Justice was the presentation offered from 21 to 26 July 1890, at the Theatre Royal, Leicester, with Weldon Atherstone giving every satisfaction as a 'cool and forcible villain', and September saw him at the Alhambra Theatre, Barrow-in-Furness, appearing in *Woman Against Woman* by Frank Harvey.

The action of this play takes place in Paris in the eighteenth century, and its first scene is laid at the house of Henri, Count de Brevannes, and his wife, Clotilde. After discussing their straitened circumstances they are informed by Alphonse Godinet, the self-styled 'honest lawyer', and his clerk, Pierre Lancette, that Ferdinand, Viscount de Brevannes, Henri's brother, has by the decease of a relative become heir to an immense fortune. Envy fills the mind of the less fortunate relatives, and the countess devises a plan to obtain possession of the money. In fact, her suggestion to the lonely Ferdinand to enter a monastery and give his legacy to his needy brother had almost succeeded when, at the critical moment, he suspects ulterior motives and announces his intention to marry Louise Perrot, who proves herself to be the heroine of the piece; and consequently incurs the hatred of a designing woman and an equally unscrupulous husband. In the next act we are introduced to the *bal masqué*, in which the graceful movements of the dancers prove a pleasing diversion. The lawyer, Godinet, comes to enjoy the fun, little suspecting that it is his clerk, Lancette – who, for some unaccountable reason, has assumed for the nonce female attire – with whom he has been carrying on an innocent flirtation. In the midst of the complications which ensue, the viscountess, believing that she is with her husband, is driven from the ballroom to the house of the Duc de Grandcour, and there the latter is surprised in his evil designs by the injured husband, who wounds the Duc de Grandcour with his sword, and avows his intention of killing his (supposed) erring wife. On second thought, however, he causes her to be taken to the prison of the Madelonottes, and the hopes of the viscountess yet to attain her ends are raised. Pathetic in the extreme are the scenes which follow, and ultimately Ferdinand's love for his wife compels him to believe in her innocence; taking her from prison, the pair are reunited. Of course the rage of the defeated count and countess knows no bounds, and the hatred of the latter for her sister-in-law stimulates her to endeavour to prove that Ferdinand has gone mad. However, in the end virtue triumphs, vice assumes its proper place and all ends well. Mr Weldon Atherstone played the Duc de Grandcour.

The census taken in April 1891 shows Thomas Weldon Atherstone with wife, Monica, and children, Thomas Frederick (aged two years and seven months) and Doris (born in Manchester some time in 1890 or 1891), all at 72 Effingham Street, Rotherham (very likely a theatrical lodgings). Atherstone and Monica both give their occupation as actor/comedian.

Preparations for the heavy lead in a new play, *Black Diamonds*, engaged Atherstone's close attention in April 1891, and, following a week (4–9 May) at the Theatre Royal, Birkenhead, in *Siberia*, he duly appeared in it at the Theatre Royal, Darwen, throughout the week of 11–16 May, rendering 'a fine portrayal of Cyril Slaker'.

Then, in June, it was on to Newcastle-under-Lyme, the Theatre Royal and *The Corsican Brothers* and *Othello*, which was greatly appreciated – 'Much of the success was due to the capital acting of Mr Weldon Atherstone and Mr C. H. Peeler.' In July, Atherstone was at the St James's Theatre, Manchester, making 'an excellent Count Danella in *Mr Barnes of New York*.

While playing at the latter venue as Paolo Macari, the political spy and assassin in *Called Back* – whom he made as diabolical a personage as the dramatist could have meant him to be – he had the misfortune, after the murder of Antony March in the prologue of the drama, to run the assassin's dagger into his own knee. It was reported that 'Mr Atherstone had the wound bound up, and very pluckily continued the impersonation'.

In *The Era* of 19 December 1891, there appeared the
following inserted notice:

> Mr Weldon Atherstone,
> as Gloster and Isaac of York,
> Miss Monica Kelly (Mrs W. A.) thanks
> Balsir Chatterton, Esq. for offer of Re-engagement
> as Patsie Blake, 'The English Rose.' Address, Theatre
> Royal, Kidderminster.

Weldon Atherstone began the year 1892 as business
manager of the South Company of Mr John F. Preston's
March tour of *Amy Robsart* at the Gaiety, Brighton. By
April, he was once more 'at liberty' for 'head or special
parts'.

It was not until June 1892 that *The English Rose*
began to bloom, but by 30 July it was emitting the
sweet perfume of success. Immense success in its sixth
week in Liverpool. Immense success for Monica Kelly as
Patsy Blake. Immense success for Weldon Atherstone as
Captain MacDonnell.

The Liverpool press was unanimous in its praise.

Said *The Liverpool Daily Post*: 'A large audience
assembled to greet ... *The English Rose*. The cast is
an exceedingly strong one. The realistic situations are
given with commendable force. Nothing is left to be
desired.' Said *The Liverpool Courier*: '*The English Rose*
bids fair to prove a great success. Production in every
sense satisfactory.' Said *The Liverpool Mercury*: 'The
piece is presented with considerable point and force by
a competent company. Staging and scenery are alike
capital.'

From 8 August to 13 August, *The English Rose*
ran at the Theatre Royal, Wigan. *The Era* reports
that 'Captain Macdonnell in the hands of Mr Weldon
Atherstone is an admirable performance', and 'Miss
Monica Kelly makes the most of Patsy Blake'.

Commencing 29 August 1892 at Portsmouth was an important production of the spectacular new Indian drama *Love and Duty*. The play moved on to the Theatre Royal, Jersey, where the depiction of stirring scenes of the Sepoy Mutiny made a great impact. Atherstone sustained well the role of the rajah, and Monica that of Josephine. Encores of the snake dances by the Juanita Nautch troupe were vociferously demanded, and a detachment of the Yorkshire Regiment added the utmost realism to the mutiny scene. The authoress of the play, Mrs Henry Wylde, who happened to be on a visit to the island, was led before the curtain 'in response to an emphatic call' and was given a great ovation.

The Era of 22 October 1892 saw Weldon Atherstone, having completed his spell in *Love and Duty* at Jersey's Theatre Royal, advertising again in its pages his availability.

The year 1893 was, so far as the Atherstones were concerned, an unremarkable one. The plays in which Weldon appeared were *Jane Shore, Ivanhoe, Kenilworth* and *The Hand of Justice*.

Jane Shore was played at Rotherham, Bishop Auckland, South Shields, Lichfield, Brighton, Bournemouth, West Bromwich and at the New Theatre Royal, Aston, where Monica Kelly was in the cast; *Ivanhoe* at Rotherham, South Shields (where Atherstone gave a powerful and much-applauded rendering of the character of Isaac), Jarrow, Aston and Bournemouth, where the proceedings were varied when, at a matinée on Wednesday 21 November, Paderewski gave a pianoforte recital to a crowded and enthusiastic audience; Scott's *Kenilworth* was also presented, as well as *The Hand of Justice*, at Jarrow in July, by Miss Georgie Walton's Company, which included both Weldon Atherstone and Monica Kelly.

In December, at the Theatre Royal, West Bromwich, the curtain for the year 1893 was brought down on *Jane Shore* and *The Hand of Justice*.

At the Art Gallery, Newcastle-on-Tyne, from 19 to 24 February 1894, Weldon Atherstone made a successful appearance with John F. Preston's Company in *The Three Musketeers*. Moving under the wing of Messrs Dottridge and Longden's Company, he entrained in April for Dudley, where, in *The King of Crime*, at the Colosseum Theatre, he was to contrive admirably to express the craven fear of the miser Gandelu's son, Simon.

In the November of 1894, he accepted the offer from Messrs Miller & Elliston's Company of a part in their production of George R. Sims and Henry Pettitt's *In the Ranks*, always a popular drama north of the Tweed, and duly appeared in it at Glasgow's Royal Princess's Theatre, where a critic found his performance as 'the Hop Picker' 'worthy of special mention'.

That year, 1894, saw the birth in Dublin of Weldon and Monica's second son, William Gordon. A happy event, but, sadly, the first cracks were beginning to show in the matrimonial wallpaper. The partnership of Weldon and Monica was not to survive all that much longer.

Early in Atherstone's 1895 calendar of engagements came *The Indian Mutiny*, at the Theatre Royal, Cradley Heath, from 11 to 16 February. In April he opened at the Queen's Theatre, Long Acre, in its Easter attraction, *The Famine*. The play was of that sensational type which pleases the occupants of the pit and gallery. Love and betrayal are the main themes upon which the action turns, and when the wedding party is abruptly terminated by the advent of the betrayed heroine upon the scene, the feelings of the audience are allowed full play. The conspiracy which leads to a fight for freedom at a lunatic asylum is brimful of sensation, and the attack on the prison van affords a character sketch which the spectators heartily enjoy. Atherstone appears to great advantage as Vincent O'Connor in the prologue, and proves himself a master of pathetic expression when afterwards – fifteen years afterwards – as the young soldier John O'Connor, he displays a welcome energy of style and gallantry of bearing. His was said to be a highly praiseworthy effort.

The Famine was still playing in 1896 – at The Spa, Harrogate; Morton's Theatre, Greenwich; the New Royal County Theatre, Reading; and the Theatre Royal, Cardiff.

In February 1896, Monica was rewarded by a perfect storm of applause having played Kathleen O'Connor in William Travers' Irish classic *Kathleen Mavourneen*, revived by the Kennedy Miller Company at the Queen's Theatre, Dublin. First produced in London at the Pavilion Theatre in February 1862, described as 'the Beautiful Irish Comedy in Three Acts', it was to achieve consistent popularity in Britain and the United States until well into the twentieth century.

A traditional wise woman has predicted that the lovely Kathleen O'Connor will one day become a 'fine lady'. Squire Bernard Pinlimmon and his sister Dorothy call at the O'Connor farmhouse. Bernard clearly entertains feelings for Kathleen, and she is attracted to him. There is, however, a fly in the ointment of romance. Kathleen has a conscience about her long-standing friend Terry O'Moore, who would, she knows, be seriously distressed if she were to marry the squire. Dorothy makes Kathleen the present of a fine cloak, which Kathleen puts on, imagining herself with the nobleman at the county ball. And a letter arrives containing a ring and a proposal of marriage from the noble Pinlimmon. Terry comes on the scene, sees the cloak and ring, and, believing them to be suitable wedding gifts from the gentry, asks her to name the day.

Act Two takes place in a handsome apartment in the Pinlimmon mansion. Kathleen is now a rich man's wife, but she has not, it transpires, found happiness, for her husband finds her an embarrassment when in company. It is now that Pinlimmon learns that as a result of foolish investments he is financially ruined. His one hope of salvation is to marry a wealthy woman, a Miss Onslow. He informs Kathleen that their marriage is illegal, because the priest who conducted the ceremony was a paid impostor, and he writes her a letter offering her an annuity if she will depart. She faints and as she does so Father O'Cassidy appears, revives her and tells her that *he* performed the wedding, substituting himself for the impostor engaged by Pinlimmon.

Hearing how his scheme went wrong, Pinlimmon is enraged and hires a man known as Black Rody to murder Kathleen at a desolate spot, making it look as if her coach had been attacked. Black Rody is to be sure to dig Kathleen's grave first. Having dug the grave, Black Rody and his accomplices await their victim. She and Pinlimmon enter, their coach having broken down. Pinlimmon walks on, pretending to be reconnoitring. Rody tells Kathleen that her husband has paid for her death. The two accomplices seize her, but the broken-hearted though ever-vigilant Terry O'Moore emerges from the rocky landscape. There is a fight. Terry kills Rody and hurls the two accomplices off the cliff. He then comforts the lady, whom not until now did he recognise as his own Kathleen. When Squire Pinlimmon returns there is a confrontation. He and Terry fight. Pinlimmon is killed. Soldiers suddenly appear, and arrest Terry for murder.

Act Three begins in a prison, where Father O'Cassidy speaks to the governor of Terry's unblemished reputation. When Kathleen comes to bid him farewell she blames herself for what has happened and vows never to love another. The dreaded execution bell sounds and the governor leads Kathleen gently away.

The scene then changes to the O'Connor cottage, where Kathleen is asleep on a chair. She awakens. It was all a dream. Terry is heard singing outside. When he enters he asks for Kathleen's answer, which is 'Yes'. Country folk assemble in holiday attire for the announcement of the wedding. Kathleen shows Terry Pinlimmon's letter proposing marriage, and when Pinlimmon duly appears among the merrymakers Terry courteously declines his proposal on Kathleen's behalf. Pinlimmon, not in the least discommoded, tells them his proffered engagement ring may be taken as a wedding gift: they are at liberty to sell it and use the money to secure Terry O'Moore's farm. Terry then addresses the audience: 'I venture to say you're glad I've got my Kathleen and that she gave me such a favourable answer to the question I asked her on St Patrick's Eve.'

In June and July, Weldon Atherstone was 'at Liberty', and advertising in *Era* for a good autumn tour.

In August 1896, he had secured, at the Grand Theatre and Opera House, Derby, the role of Jasper Woodleigh, the villainous nephew of Sir Geoffrey Woodleigh, in Arthur Jefferson's *The World's Verdict*.

A critic in *The Era,* writing about this play, observed, 'Melodrama with the strongest possible flavour of sensationalism never fails to satisfy a large section of those audiences on which suburban theatres depend for support.' And the *Hull Daily Mail*, of Tuesday 18 August 1896, under the heading 'The Maniac's Knife', had this to say:

'Shriek!' 'Laugh!' Do everything that a maniac would do. If the knowledge of a maniac's shriek or laugh is limited then those whose intelligence on that score be proscribed should go to the Hull Theatre Royal this week. The fourth act of *The World's Verdict* is made morbid by the staging of what is termed the 'Maniac's den.' There is a skull, crossbones, and a maniac in a den. Here takes place such a horrible scene that last night a woman rushed out of the Theatre into Paragon Street looking hysterical, and exclaiming that she would never visit the theatre again. What a tribute to theatrical realism!

The World's Verdict was still playing – at the Prince of Wales' Theatre, Great Grimsby – in October, but in *The Era* of 17 October 1896, Weldon Atherstone is advertising his liberty at Christmas to accept Heavy Lead, &c., but *The World's Verdict* continued at the Theatre Royal, Longton; the Theatre Royal, Oldham; the Theatre Royal, Barnsley; the Grand Theatre, Birmingham; and Morton's Theatre, Greenwich.

Coming events cast their shadows before them. From the United States came the new Edison 'Vitascope', which showed waves breaking on the beach, dancing routines and the live blow exchanges of boxing matches. These 'flickers' were the result of the work of Thomas Edison in the USA and the brothers Louis and Auguste Lumière in France. The vaudeville theatres were beginning to buy the sixteen-frame-per-second film pictures and the machines to project them. Here then, in 1896, was the future destroyer of the myriad little provincial theatres that were the lifeblood of artists such as Weldon Atherstone, and the creator of the hundreds of cinemas which superseded them.

The early days of the new year, 1897, were scarcely auspicious, the issues of *The Era* for 30 January and 13 February both containing intimations of Mr Weldon Atherstone's liberty to accept invitations to undertake 'Heavy Lead, &c.'

Happily, by April he was accommodated. A part had been offered and accepted in *The Streets of London*, said to be by far the most popular of Dion Boucicault's series of dramas. Occupying the stage of Her Majesty's Theatre, Carlisle, in April – and subsequently those of the Theatre Royal, York, and the Theatre Royal, North Shields – with Atherstone hissed and howled at, supplying an obviously sufficiently and satisfactorily villainous Gideon Bloodgood, it was achieving good business. The inclusion in the performances of local volunteers – the fire brigade at Carlisle, to fight the grand final conflagration scene at

Seven Dials, and twenty local children at North Shields, to perform, in the fourth act, the Urchins' Street Ballet – lent special interest to the productions. The play was described as 'a thrilling drama, in which fine, noble, and manly sentiment is combined with tragic and startling incident, an immensity of real comedy, fun and pathos'. It was received with uniform enthusiasm in May, at Her Majesty's Theatre, Aberdeen; in June, at the Royal Osborne Theatre, Manchester, and the Theatre Royal, Halifax; and in September at the Theatre Royal, Jersey.

Weldon's wife, appearing without him, was making a capital Katey Malone in the Irish play about Lord Edward Fitzgerald, *Lord Edward; or '98*, at the Liverpool Rotunda in July 1897. The audience's frequent applause showed their high appreciation of her performance. Later that same month she appeared, again *sans* Weldon, in *The Irishman* at the Rotunda. It was a sensational drama which had been performed for over 3,000 nights in various parts of the United Kingdom, and had proved popular as far away as the United States, Canada and Australia.

The year was brought to a close with *The Hand of Time* by John Glendinning, staged at the Theatre Royal, Darlington, from 20 to 25 December. The plot was not of a mystifying order. The opening scene reveals the Bowling Green Inn at Withington-by-the-Sea, where Harry Lyndon and Frank Lyle, two young farmers and friends, and other personages are engaged in the pastime of bowls. Harry has been selling stock and is on the spree, flinging money away. While in his cups he is of an irascible disposition, and he quarrels with Frank. In the course of the struggle the latter falls over the cliffs, and is supposed by Lyndon to have been killed. Stung with remorse, Harry Lyndon determines to leave the locality, but not before he has exchanged garments with a tramp whom he has befriended in former days. A ghastly deed follows close upon the supposed crime: the tramp,

Ben Keogh, is murdered and knocked into the sea by Tetlow, a brewer on the verge of bankruptcy who has followed Harry Lyndon, intending to rob him. Finding no money upon Ben Keogh, Tetlow pushes the tramp's body into the sea, and a blind boy, Terence, who was accompanying Keogh, calls in vain for him to return.

In Act Two, Ben's body, battered by the rocks out of all recognition, is picked up and taken for that of Lyndon; and through the scheming of Tetlow, aided by Bulger, a stupid fellow who thinks himself a born detective, a charge of murder is preferred against Frank Lyle, who was found alive at the foot of the cliff and in possession of Harry's money, which had been entrusted to him for safe keeping.

The proceedings of the subsequent act take place in London, where Harry is living in obscurity in the East End. On hearing that a travelling quack doctor, named à Beckett, is in danger of being convicted of the murder he thinks he has committed, Harry resolves to return and give himself up.

Act Four takes us back to Withington, to the Old Manor Farm, where Harry Lyndon's wife is mourning for him as dead. When the house is all quiet for the night, Harry finds his way in and has a conversation with his little daughter, who does not recognise him. He retires as Frank Lyle, having escaped from prison, rushes in, only to be retaken almost immediately by Tetlow and Bulger. Harry reappears for a moment at the window and is seen by Frank alone, and the two men, each supposing the other dead, severally think the other to be an apparition.

The curtain in the closing act rises on the morning of Frank's execution. Harry has again disappeared, having met with an accident, but he recovers in time to try and get to the prion and save Frank. He is prevented in this by Tetlow, but manages to send the blind boy with a note, which falls into the hands of Harry's wife, Madge. She tries to obtain admission to the prison, but is stopped by Bulger, and at last, to gain time, she enters the old clock tower, climbs out of the window, up to the clock, and pulls back the large hand, thus delaying the execution long enough to enable Harry and the other characters to save Frank.

For the part of Seth Tetlow, Mr Weldon Atherstone, in cold, calculating style, expressed the character well.

The year 1898 opened up with Atherstone, in January, at the Queen's Theatre, Longton, in Sims and Pettitt's *In the Ranks*, and the following month he was in Belfast, at the Theatre Royal, playing Captain Lionel Anstey in Brandon Ellis' *The City Outcast*, performed with James Bell's specially selected company. As its title indicates, the piece is of the sensational school, and from start to finish abounds in exciting and thrilling incidents.

The whole play centres on Arthur Beechly, the child and sole heir of Sir Arthur Beechly. An adventurer and cousin of Sir Arthur named Captain Lionel Anstey is determined to do away with young Arthur Beechly, who is his only bar to the possession of the estates, and by making promises of love and marriage to Mysah Feerah, an Indian nurse, he obtains her assistance in his vile object. The child, while playing on the bank of a river, topples into the water and is supposed to be lost. Having, in his opinion, secured his objective, Anstey proves false to his promises to Feerah, and treats her with scorn. She, in a spirit of revenge, reveals the truth; the boy is not dead, though a waif on the streets of London. He is recovered and restored and all ends in the way one desires. Atherstone, as the villainous Captain Anstey, had an unenviable part to fill, but he succeeded so well that the audience literally groaned him off the stage – which is to say, they greatly appreciated his efforts! Particularly impressive was, in scene one, act two, the exceedingly realistic view of St Paul's Cathedral by night, with snow falling.

In the Grand Hall at Bromley, in Kent, from 10 to

12 March 1898 Atherstone gave a fine delineation of Richard Belton, the returned convict, in *In the Ranks*. The performance was repeated in Nottingham, at the Grand Theatre, in September, and met with similar praise. Thereafter, it was staged at the Theatre Royal, Leeds (April); the Broadway Theatre, Deptford (August); the Grand Royal Theatre, Nottingham (September); the Theatre Royal, Aston (September); the Lyceum Theatre, Ipswich (October); the St George's Theatre, Burton-on-Trent (October); the Pleasure Gardens Theatre, Folkestone (November); and the Lyceum Theatre, Newport (December).

The month of June imported to Atherstone the task of mastering, or perhaps revising, yet another script, this time that of the part of Captain O'Donnell in *The English Rose*. He was to play in it at the Prince's Theatre, Accrington (June); the Alexandra Theatre, Sheffield (June); at the Broadway Theatre, Deptford (August); and at the Theatre Royal, Nottingham (September).

In March 1899 he began a series of engagements at the Lyric Theatre, Hammersmith. From 6 to 11 March he was acting in 'a specially dramatised version of Dumas' masterpiece', *The Adventures of the Count De Monte Cristo*, cast as M. Noirtier. The critique in *The Era* states, 'We cannot say that the dramatisation is a good one, but it serves its purpose.'

The play opens at the Harbour of Marseilles, where Mercedes is awaiting the arrival of her lover, Edmund Dantes, mate of the *Pharaoh*. When he arrives it appears that he has taken command of the ship through the death of the captain, and in that capacity he has had delivered to him at the island of Elba, where the ship had called, a letter from Napoleon Bonaparte to a conspirator in Marseilles. This becoming known to Baron Danglars, the supercargo of the ship, who is jealous of Dantes' promotion, and Fernand Mondego, a fisherman in love with Mercedes, they conspire against Dantes, and by informing Villefort, the *Procureur de Roi*, of the existence of the letter they contrive to have Dantes arrested on the eve of his wedding and taken to the Château D'If. Fourteen years elapse between the prologue and act one and we are now shown the adjoining cells in the prison occupied by Dantes and the Abbé Faria. The prisoners are able to communicate with each other, and the dying Abbé acquaints Dantes with the existence of the buried treasure on the island of Monte Cristo. The Abbé dies, and Dantes, hearing the prison warders express their intention of putting the body in a sack and throwing it into the sea, resolves to escape by placing himself in the sack and being cast over the ramparts in place of the corpse. This he does successfully, and in a well-planned mechanical change of scene we see the sack thrown into the water. Dantes rips open the sack with his knife, and is saved by clinging to a rock, from which he proclaims, 'The world is mine.'

In Act Two Dantes, in pursuit of his vengeance against his trio of persecutors, masquerades as the Abbé Busoni and Johannes, a Jew. He discovers that Villefort is conspiring against the king, and hands him over to the soldiery, but Villefort, in order to escape conviction, kills himself.

After a lapse of five years, Act Three introduces us to the house of De Moncerf, the Fernand Mondego of the prologue, who has married Mercedes. They have a son, Albert, whose life has been saved some years before by the Count of Monte Cristo, and on his invitation the count pays De Moncerf a visit. He meets Mercedes, who is struck with the resemblance to Dantes. The count denounces Mondego, who in a short duel is mortally wounded, and dies. Albert is enraged, demanding satisfaction, and a meeting is arranged for the next day, when Mercedes intervenes and reveals to Dantes and Albert that which has hitherto been kept a secret: that Albert is the son of herself and Dantes. Nevertheless, the intending duellists meet in the forest of Fontainebleau, but, instead of fighting, Albert apologises to his father. Danglars, who is present as Albert's second, makes an insolent remark, at which Dantes goads Danglars into fury, and a duel takes place between them. Danglars is killed, and the curtain falls, Dantes' vengeance being satisfied.

For six days from Monday 13 March 1899, Atherstone was at the Lyric appearing in *The Work Girl* in the role of Silas Sephton, a villain who does not stop short at murder, and who, in the course of his career, has acquired a mansion in Park Lane.

The bill at the Lyric from 20 to 25 March was *The King of Crime*, Atherstone reprising his old part as Simon Gandelu, who betrays Jules Lemaire, alias Captain Hercules, leader of a gang of robbers, to the police.

The last of Weldon Atherstone's Lyric run was *The Great World of London*, curtain up on 3 April 1899. The main sensation of this play was a murder in a railway carriage, and great interest was provoked by a realistic scene of the Salvation Army shelter in the Mile End Road. Moreover, the cast was an unusually large one – thirty-five male and six female characters – made up of nearly every description of person that could be met with in London from east to west. Atherstone's person was John Meredith, his interpretation, somewhat unusually, tepidly adjudged as merely 'satisfactory'.

Thereafter, Mr Weldon Atherstone was euphemistically 'at liberty' until, on 17 April, he picked up the part of the crafty and complaisant squireen of Corry Kinchela in *The Shaughraun*, at the Elephant and Castle. This is one of the best, if not the best, of Dion Boucicault's Irish plays.

He was engaged in May at the Alexandra Theatre, Sheffield, as the daring villain Jacob Cuthbert in *Humanity*, and in June he was at the St Helens Theatre Royal and Opera House playing Mark Harley in *The*

Power of Gold, an American drama by Walter Sanford, the plot of which hinged upon the strained relations between two brothers, Mark Harley and Paul Judson. Set scenes included the exterior of the Foundling Hospital, the interior of a lunatic asylum, and the Regent Canal by night. The villainess finds her doom in a poisoned bath prepared for the heroine. The chief role is that of Lady Brandon, an adventuress who assumes the name and position of her former mistress, who is supposed dead, and there is the dark-skinned, snakish and wily Malay doctor, Hadgi Zambra. The play moved on to the Oldham Colosseum, the Sheffield Theatre Royal and the Theatre Royal, Halifax, in July.

The Era of Saturday 8 July 1899 published the following:

Tonight, 125th Night of uninterrupted success.
No weather too hot, as proved on June 24,
with an open-air fête to contend with
at St. Helens. Receipts, £35 1s. 3d.
No opposition too strong, as shown on last Saturday,
during the height of the election fever
at Colosseum, Oldham. Receipts, £48 4s. 3d.

Seven Political Meetings in the town same night.
Managers desirous of making money will Book.
Miss Ethel Van Praagh's
Latest Dramatic Success
The Greatest of all Scenic Productions
'THE POWER OF GOLD.'
A Human Drama, in Four Acts,
of absorbing interest,
abounding in Thrilling Incidents,
Startling Situations, and Replete with Comic Relief.
Double Calls after each Act.
Company of Artistes known to Every Manager:-
Ethel Van Praagh, Charles Girdlestone, Frank Ayrton,

Weldon Atherstone, Madge Seymour, Beatrice Deighton,
Elizabeth Earle, Tom Ronald, Harry Sydney,
Hans Ormonde, Elsie Hammond, William Victor.

It is to be noted that a new name appears in the company: that of Elizabeth Earle.

She is accorded favourable notice by the critic attending the Sheffield performance of *The Power of Gold*. He writes in *The Era* of 15 July 1899, 'Miss Elizabeth Earle wins the sympathies of the audience.' And when the play moves on to the Theatre Royal, Halifax, at the end of July, a critic writes, 'Miss Elizabeth Earle is eminently successful as the persecuted heroine, and gives a very realistic performance.' At the Theatre Royal, Wigan, in August, she is again singled out: 'Miss Elizabeth Earle's rendition of the persecuted Meg Judson deserves the warmest commendation.'

Elizabeth Earle was twenty-four, having been born in America in 1875. Her mother, Josephine, was also American, born around 1841 at Taneytown, Maryland. Her father was George Earle, a commercial traveller.

At the time of the 1891 census, Josephine Earle and her sixteen-year-old daughter Bessie were living in England, boarding at 89 Edith Grove, Chelsea. She was then giving her profession as 'teacher of Expressive School' and that of her daughter as 'reciter'.

In *The Morning Post* of 17 June 1891 was published the following notice:

Miss Synge's Annual Concert (under distinguished patronage) will take place on Tuesday, June 23, at St. James's Hall (Banqueting Hall) Regent Street entrance to commence at three o'clock. The following artistes will kindly assist Herr and Madam Schulz, zither and cymbalo &c. Madlle Noemi Lorenzi, soprano; Miss Ida Audain, harp; Mr John Pitts, violin; Signor Peruzzi, violoncello; Miss Bessie Earle, recitation; Two of Miss Synge's pupils will make their début. Pianists and conductors, Miss Synge Mr F. Sewell Southgate.

In the May of the following year Bessie had graduated to the legitimate stage, appearing, according to *The Era* (14 May 1892), at the Grand Theatre, Birmingham, in a round of Shakespearian plays – *Hamlet*, *The Merchant of Venice*, *Romeo and Juliet*, *Othello* and *Macbeth*. The company included Mr Fisher White and Miss Elizabeth Earle.

October saw Bessie on stage at St George's Hall in the Vaudeville Amateur Dramatic Club's presentation of Sir Charles L. Young's *Jim the Penman*, earning *The Era*'s critical comment that 'Miss Elizabeth Earle was acceptable as Agnes Ralston'.

Mother was still making periodic theatrical appearances, too. *The Era* of 11 December 1897 observed, 'At the Brighton Aquarium Mrs Josephine Earle was an admirable Mrs Ur Snaffies.' The play was a comedy, *Retiring*.

Filling in the 1901 census, Josephine was now giving the date of her birth as about 1848, and her age as fifty-three. She is living in Parliament Hill Mansions with Joseph Fisher White, actor, and Edith R. White, actress. He is thirty-five and she is twenty-nine. Josephine gives her occupation as that of costume designer.

Josephine Clifton Earle died in the presence of her daughter in the flat that she was sharing with her at No. 8 Clifton Gardens, Prince of Wales Road, Battersea, on 22 February 1905. Her death, due to phthisis and asthenia, was certified by Dr P. R. Dodwell.

It was in the summer of 1899, in the month of July, that Bessie came to play in *The Power of Gold* with Ethel Van Praagh's Company at the Theatre Royal, Sheffield. Fate was set to cross the ill-starred paths of Elizabeth and Weldon. Elizabeth won the sympathies of the audience as the persecuted heroine. Weldon did effective work as Mark Harley.

In September 1899, Atherstone was back at the Lyric playing in an old Lyric stock favourite, *True as Steel*. John Inglesant stands in the dock falsely convicted of murder; he escapes from penal servitude, makes a fortune in diamonds and returns twenty years later to even things up and undermine all the efforts of a remorseless villain. Atherstone takes the part of Jabez Hartland.

Also at the Lyric in September, he was given a part in *The Gipsy Earl*. The work of George R. Sims, it was a drama requiring a number of specially engaged artistes in addition to an already large stock company. The piece was interlarded with many Romany phrases. The old mill scene was very well staged, and the escape of Pharoah Lee by means of the mill's sails was enthusiastically applauded. Weldon was distinctly good as Anselo Lovell, a blind Gipsy.

Still at the Lyric in October, he undertook the small part of Hiram Webster in *The Fatal Card*. Set in the saloon bar of the Three Stars and at the Foot of the Rockies, it was reminiscent of one of Bret Harte's early stories. In the concluding act George Marrable, 'the drunkard of the Rockies', gives up his life to save Gerald Austen.

November 1899 brought *The Middleman* by Henry Arthur Jones to the Lyric. It was not the kind of fare to which the theatre's audiences were accustomed, but it proved an all-round success. In the early acts the inventor Cyrus Blenkarn is a simple, unbusinesslike man, who has no thought of anything but his inventions and his adoration for his two daughters. It is only when he discovers that his favourite offspring has been betrayed by the son of his employer that his nature changes and he becomes the keen moneymaker in the hope of revenging himself against his late principal, Joseph Chandler, the pottery manufacturer and middleman who has thriven on the fruits of Cyrus Blenkarn's industry. Atherstone's part is that of the time-serving and obsequious Batty Todd.

At liberty for 'leading business' in late November, Atherstone was fixed up by mid-December at Preston, where he assumed the Thespian identity of one Horace O'Neil in *Passion of Life* at the Prince's Theatre, in which play he continued at the Theatre Royal, Nuneaton, from 1 January to 6 January 1900.

5
Last Stages
1900–1910

From 19 February 1900, Atherstone was at the Crown
Theatre in Peckham High Street. The piece being played
there was a new sensational and patriotic drama, *Send
Her Victorious: A Tale of the Transvaal* by Sutton Vane.
It was very spectacular, featuring an attack by Boers
on an armoured train, with real Maxim guns in action.
There were, too, most vivid scenes of battle, and of a
military band and parade.

Still at the Crown, Peckham, from 5 to 10 March 1900
there was presented *With Flying Colours* by Seymour
Hicks and Fred G. Latham, in which Weldon gave
his usual smooth performance as the urbane Sir John
Derrick. He continued at the Crown into the next week,
with *Women and Wine* by Shirley and Landeck.

During the first week in April he was at the Paragon,
Mile End Road, in *The Flower Girl, or, Life in the East
End*, a playlet by John East and Cayley Calvert, the stage
peopled by an assorted crowd of costers, their donahs,
Salvation Army lassies, larrikins and fly kiddies. The
villain, Richard Hawke, otherwise Flash Dick (Weldon
Atherstone), hearing that Ethel, a flower girl, was about
to become an heiress, set to work at once wooing her,
and, although she was already the accepted fiancée of the

Revd Franklin, succeeded in winning her. Flash Dick then arranged a phoney wedding ceremony, well knowing that once her chastity had been outraged he would be in a position to dictate terms. By the next scene Ethel has given birth to an illegitimate child. On being told that her offspring had been born out of wedlock, obsessed with guilt and remorse, she becomes wild and reckless. Acting on information received from Dicky Dials, the Revd Franklin tracks Ethel down. The muscular parson chances upon Flash Dick in the Mile End Wastes, and the two have a prolonged struggle. When news of the flower girl's inheritance becomes a reality, Flash Dick holds their child to ransom. Ethel refuses to meet his demands and he attempts to murder her, only to be interrupted by the opportune arrival of the police. Flash Dick turns at bay, and puts a bullet through his brain. The Revd Franklin, although unable to countenance the flower girl's infidelity by marrying her, agrees that she and the baby shall become his responsibility and that 'life hereafter will be forever peaceful and free from care'. Curtain.

It was not until 4 June that Atherstone was at the Peckham Crown again. It was the holidays and brought out an old favourite, Charles Reade's *It's Never too Late to Mend*. A holiday gesture in the form of a reduction in the price of seats helped to bring crowded houses to the Crown, and Weldon Atherstone imported the necessary quota of dignity to the role of Isaac Levi and demonstrated that he could successfully simulate the passion required to make the cursing of Meadows effective.

Under the Red Cross, by that 'well-known wielder of the willow' G. B. Nichols, formerly a prominent member of the Somersetshire County Eleven, provided Weldon's next opportunity, at the Gordon Theatre, Stoke, in mid-July. Nichols had sought his inspiration in the South African war, and the story recalls a period when every item of news from the Transvaal was awaited with anxious forebodings. In act one of the play's four – 'A Farm near the Frontier' – the first blood of the war is represented as being shed when Stephen Steiner, a renegade, shoots John Forrest, an English farmer in the Transvaal whose daughter has angered him by refusing his offer of marriage. Of course a good deal happens before the way is made clear for the charming heroine, Ethel Forrest, to wed the man of her choice, Frank Grahame, who incurs the implacable hatred of Steiner and consequently has some hairbreadth escapes from death at the hands of that scoundrel. Atherstone did well as Dr Fred Masters, which role he repeated at the Royal County Theatre, Reading, in August, and at the Surrey in late September.

Incidentally, that August, Monica Kelly was acting at the Gordon, Stoke, doing well as Molly in *The Irishman*. The break-up of the Atherstone/Anderson marriage was by this time well established. In 1901 Weldon was living with his two sons, Thomas (twelve) and William (seven), in a boarding house at No. 7 The Grove, Hammersmith. His daughter Doris (ten) remained in the custody of her mother but was then a boarder at the Convent of Mercy, 4 College Street, Nottingham. Monica Anderson being a devout Roman Catholic, there was no question of a divorce. There is no clue as to the cause of the separation, but, taking into account certain future happenings, an educated guess might suggest the possibility of morbid jealousy being the root cause of the trouble.

February 1902 found Atherstone at the Opera House, Coventry, in *A Fatal Crown*, a historical drama, the chief character in which was the ill-fated Lady Jane Grey, who, for seven days, figured as queen of this realm.

June and July were busy months. First of all, at Her Majesty's Theatre, Dundee, *The Octoroon*, Boucicault's famous American drama, frankly theatrical in style. The exciting sale of the slaves, the murder of Paul, the discovery of his murderer by means of the camera, the great fight between Jacob McClusky and the Indian chief; all were features of absorbing interest to a popular audience, and Atherstone quickly attracted admiration by his incisive and powerful acting. In look and gesture he was alike excellent, and his controversies with Salem Scudder, as well as his memorable fight with Wah-ne Tee, were splendidly managed.

Next came two plays, *The Unknown* and *Kathleen Mavourneen*. Then to Her Majesty's Theatre, Aberdeen, 23–28 June, for *The Octoroon*; back to Dundee for *The Shaughraun*, followed, in the week of 7–12 July, by *My Sweetheart*, the longevity of which few modern plays have enjoyed. There had been very few, if any, week evenings in which it had not been performed in some part of the world, and it was to a large extent the forerunner of the many musical plays which had since become popular. In this comedy, blended with pathos and enhanced by music, Weldon gave what was hailed as 'an outstandingly strong and dramatic performance as Joe Shotwell, the "old sport", playing with grimly suggestive humour, and filling the role with abundance of artistic and realistic detail'. Despite his small part, he had the satisfaction of gaining some of the heartiest applause of the evening.

For the week of 14–19 July, beside an excellent repeat performance of *East Lynne*, Her Majesty's, Dundee, presented also the first night of a piquant little new play by Fred A. Hoare, *A Guard of Honour*. If in *East Lynne* Atherstone was not as enthusiastic a lover as one might have wished, he was unquestionably more successful later on as the cynical, mocking, Francis Levison.

On 15 July, *Fun on the Bristol* was put on at Her Majesty's, Dundee. 'It was by no means the freshest or most refined of American "pantomimical farces", but it was at least a pleasant variation from what has obtained during the past week or two. *Fun on the Bristol* really is, despite the slightly "chestnut" age of the

jokes, a laughter-producing piece.' Weldon Atherstone
made a fine Count Menaggio. From 21–26 July, his
last week in Dundee for 1902, Atherstone played, with
great approbation, the scheming and vengeful Cardinal
Richelieu in *The Three Musketeers*.

In June 1903, after a fortnight's closure for renovation
and redecoration, Her Majesty's reopened. The place
was much brightened. The entrance hall, staircase and
walls of the auditorium and the proscenium had all been
repainted and redecorated in white, cream and gold. The
electric lighting, too, had undergone improvement.

The Two Orphans, the play with which the theatre
re-opened on 22 June, was not only French in plot but
also in construction, which is to say that it was intense
and emotional. The feelings were wrung for the woes of
the poor, blind Louisa and the lame Pierre and shocked
by the cruelty of the demoralised Le Frochard and her
bullying son, Jacques. The inspiring and enlivening
features of this straightforward and honest melodrama
were the comicalities of Picard, a voluble, volatile valet;
the brave steadfastness of the Chevalier de Vaudray;
and the kindliness of the doctor and the superior of
Saltpêtrière. The drama has its origin in the period
when the French Revolution was fomenting. Its moral
illustrates the profligacy of the aristocracy at the time,
and the generous, brave-hearted bourgeoisie. The
scene where the chivalrous Vaudray rescues the orphan
Henrietta from the Marquis de Oréales is perhaps the
most striking of the lot. Atherstone, as Jacques, played
the idle, bullying rascal to perfection; his 'dash and go'
being first-class.

In July Weldon acted successfully in *The Ticket-of-
Leave Man* at Her Majesty's before bidding farewell to
Dundee.

August 1903 saw him in Manchester, at the Regent.
A new play: *The Temptress* by William Steen. Another
stirring melodrama – a vitriol-throwing outrage,

revolvers, kidnapping and a knife fight terminating in the death of the villain, Lucas Denbeigh. He is, of course, Weldon Atherstone. He is the chief of a gang of forgers, and the accomplice in crime of the charming temptress. Among his other accomplishments, Denbeigh possesses the faculty of mesmerism. Conceiving a violent passion for a lovely girl named Marion Fordyce, he forces her under hypnotic influence to declare her love for him, and all but consummates his design of marriage, wafting her to the nuptial brink. Weldon's interpretation of his role was, as usual, clever, vigorous and impossible to fault.

The Temptress moved on in December to the Theatre Royal, Leeds, and was playing in South and North Shields in January and February 1904. In August he was bringing to life yet another villain, Geoffrey Warden, in *The Female Swindler* at St Helen's, which role he repeated in Warrington, Smethwick, Liverpool and Nelson in October, November and December 1905.

March 1906 saw him at the Ealing Hippodrome, as Colonel Charlestown in a military spectacle called *The Britisher*.

On New Year's Day, Tuesday 1 January 1907, he achieved a really fine portrayal of Napoleon in 'a brilliant musical play', *The Duchess of Danzig*, put on at the Chelmsford Corn Exchange. In April he was a striking Friar Laurence in *Romeo and Juliet* at the Terriss Theatre in south-east London, and in May played in *Saved from the Sea*, at the Borough, Stratford. In July he was at the East Oxford Theatre in *Man's Enemy*, playing with easy nonchalance the part of Tom Duke. And in October 1907, he was Dr Colebrook in *Life's Sweetest Sins*, at the north London Grand.

At the Brixton Theatre the curtain went up in the week of 31 December 1907–4 January 1908 on *The Great World of London*, wherein Weldon Atherstone, as Richard Thornton, had a part that any stage villain might revel in. At the Wigan Royal Court Theatre in

July 1908, he appeared as John Jasper in *The Mystery of Edwin Drood*.

Thereafter, Atherstone's engagements seem to have been on an increasingly downhill slide. He was never a star, but he was a conscientious craftsman, a gifted and reliable actor in continuous demand by the managers of respectable suburban and provincial theatres.

At the end of April 1909, he was at the Shakespeare Theatre, Battersea, in *Revenge*. In May 1910, he was at the Bow Palace, in Bow Road, East London, committed to a short tour for Fred Moule with his play, or rather music-hall sketch, *The Grip of the Law*. After that he was at Sadler's Wells, in Roseberry Avenue, Finsbury, then at the Foresters Music Hall, in Cambridge Heath Road, Bethnal Green; the Battersea Palace, in York Road; and the Surrey Theatre, at the southern end of Blackfriars Road, Lambeth.

At the end of February 1910, a mere five months before his untimely death, Weldon Atherstone was in Hastings, at the Gaiety Theatre, taking the part of John Bowlby MP in *A Country Mouse*, which made delightful entertainment, if only as a skit upon the ways and manners of high society – that society of peers and wealthy folk which had at that time the limelight of publicity so mercilessly shed upon its little foibles and weaknesses. But, above that, the piece was a truly bright and diverting little comedy, full of broad humour and highly amusing incidents. There is humour, rich humour, in the idea of the apparently ingenuous, unsophisticated girl from the country playing simpleton so cleverly that she deceives all the clever people who are trying to take advantage of her simplicity, and in the end marries the duke. Mr Atherstone carried off his part with notably quiet force and dignity.

He had also been appearing at Brighton West Pier as Dr Candy in one of those bright and breezy farces that never grow stale, *The New Boy*, and returned to

Hastings to play at the Gaiety there in both *A Country Mouse* and *The New Boy* in March.

During the final trickle of his days Atherstone filled in with performing various recitations and monologues at third- and fourth-rate suburban London theatres.

This may account for the somewhat curious reference to him by Richard Gordon on page 111 of his *The Private Life of Dr Crippen* (2001), where, admirably imaginatively, he reconstructs the evening of Atherstone's performing days.

He writes,

> Weldon 'Anderson' the monologuist, with top hat, tails and ebony cane. Perfect tailoring was his trademark, like the black half-moons of George Robey's eyebrows, or Albert Chevalier's suit of Cockney costermonger's button-covered 'pearlies'. He did Fagin in the condemned cell from *Oliver Twist*, the music hall falling as silent as a church.
>
> 'The black stage, the cross-beam, the rope … '
> Atherstone's low voice seemed to ooze from him.
> 'All the hideous apparatus of death.'

Atherstone never penetrated the charmed circle of the West End stage. His was the world of suburban and provincial theatre. His name, virtually unknown to fashionable society, nevertheless stood well in the coin of the realm of the play-going public, especially those who delighted in the thud and blunder of sensational melodrama and awarded the convincingly villainous with hisses and howls and execrations, and heroism with frantic applause.

Although he knew nothing of it, Weldon Atherstone stood now upon the threshold of stardom and country-wide fame as central character in the black limelight of a real-life drama far more powerful than any of his three decades of make-believe. But it was an ultimate celebrity that was to cost him his life.

*

It is eightish in the evening of 16 July 1910.

In his lodgings at 14 Great Percy Street, King's Cross, the forty-seven-year-old veteran actor, dressed in his best dark-blue serge suit, is making a careful brown-paper-and-string parcel of his felt carpet slippers. He has already stowed away in the space between his body and the back of his jacket another neatly wrapped brown paper object: a somewhat sinister, lethally heavy weight of electric telegraph wire, fashioned, with convenient string loop for the wrist, into a formidable 'life preserver', or cosh.

Stepping forth into the bright and bristling Saturday night of west central London, eyes and thoughts obsessionally fixed upon the task looming before him, the actor catches a tram to Battersea. Alighting at Battersea Bridge Road, he finds himself in quiet, dark territory on the night-black lip of Battersea Park. Soft-footedly he approaches his objective, the rear of No. 8 Clifford Gardens, Prince of Wales Road. It is to the empty ground-floor flat here that the actor stealthily makes his way. So determined is he that he contrives entrance to the dark, deserted premises. Love and jealousy know not locks and bolts. He unties his parcel. Puts on his slippers. Parcels his discarded boots. Places the parcel on the mantelshelf. The slippers will make soundless his clamber up the iron staircase, so that he may surprise in the act his unsuspecting rival. He shuffles towards the back scullery door. His ear catches the sound of movement outside. He is instantly tense, alert. It happens in a fractured second. The two intruders' bodies clash and crash. Almost certainly, neither has the faintest clue who the other is. Blindly they struggle. Shots rip the air – and rip into the actor. His unknown assailant flees, to be wrapped in the eternal unknowing of the night's blackness. In the shadow of the iron staircase the actor dies.

1A. The Albert Bridge, under construction, Battersea Park.

1B. Albert Mansions, Albert Bridge Road Battersea.

1C. Battersea Street scene, Northcote Road.

1D. Battersea Old Church, St Mary's. J. M. W. Turner painted here, and William Blake is buried here.

2. Map of the Battersea area.

3. The binomial mansions (front view) – No. 8 Clifton Gardens and No. 17 Prince of Wales Road.

4. The binomial mansions (back view), showing the iron staircase.

Right: 4A. The iron stairs.

Below: 4B. The wall of Cambridge House over which the man scrambled as he fled from the scene of the murder.

5. The only known extant photograph of Thomas Weldon Atherstone or Anderson in life.

6. Elizabeth Earle, actress and mistress.

7. Thomas Frederick
Anderson, Atherstone's
elder son.

WILLIAM. ANDERSON
(SON. OF. MURDERED. MAN)

8. William Gordon
Anderson, Atherstone's
younger son.

9. Monica Kelly, Atherstone's wife.

10. 'TRUTH STRANGER THAN FICTION. JOHN BULL (holiday making): Detective stories, sensational novels? No thank you, guess I can find all the sensation I want in the papers!' Station bookstall exhibiting side-by-side posters of the Crippen and Battersea murder mysteries.

11. The opening of the inquest under coroner Mr John Troutbeck. Scene in the Battersea Coroner's Court.

Left: 12. Miss Harriet Anderson, Atherstone's sister and the first witness.

Opposite: 13. The silent witness. This stone image, carved by the owner/builder above the front door of his house in Rosenau Road, 'saw' the running murderer pass by. The head was retrieved by the author when the premises was being demolished.

14. Cambridge House School and the binomial mansions, as seen from Rosenau Road.

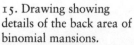

15. Drawing showing details of the back area of binomial mansions.

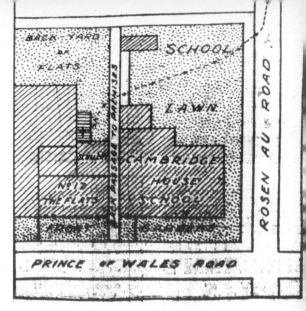

16. The lay of the land and properties viewed from the front of Prince of Wales Road.

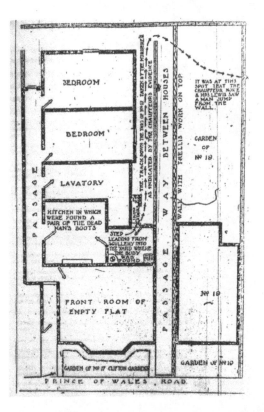

17. Ground plan of the empty ground-floor flat at the binomial mansions.

18. Edward Noice.

19. Emma Lewis.

20. Police Sergeant
William Buckley.

INSPECTOR BADCOCK
READS MISS EARL'S
STATEMENT

21. Divisional
Detective Inspector
Edward Badcock.

Left: 22. Dr Felix Charles Kempster.

Right: 23. Dr Ludwig B. Freyberger.

24. Miss Earle hiding her face in the witness box.

25. Miss Earle in the witness box, her veil lifted.

26. Elizabeth Earle – her altered aspect after her ordeal.

27. Miss Earle in her stage days.

Opposite 28. Miss Earle as she was in the beginning.

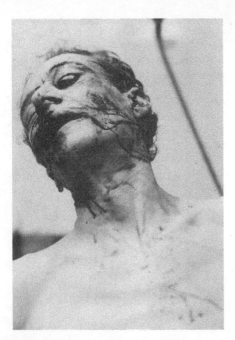

29. Official police photograph. Thomas Weldon Atherstone; his last curtain.

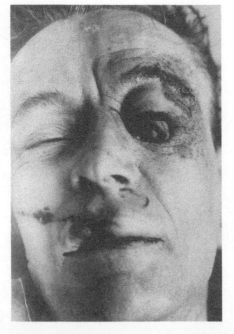

30. The final close-up.

6

Curtain Fall

Arriving at the blush-red mansion block on the green fringe of Battersea Park, Sergeant Buckley entered it by the main or front door and crossed over to the ground-floor flat. Finding it empty and securely shut, he decided to try his luck at the first-floor apartment, and duly ascended the rather splendid communal stone stair. Aloft, a thirty-five-year-old woman, Elizabeth Earle, and a twenty-one-year-old youth, Thomas Frederick Anderson, were sitting at supper in the kitchen.

The sergeant knocked at the door. Miss Earle opened it. Buckley, speaking in casual tones calculated to put Miss Earle at her ease, said, 'Good evening. We have had information that a couple of shots have been fired in one of these backyards, probably in the yard belonging to this house. Will you allow me to go down your staircase into the yard? The lower flat being empty I can't easily get through that.'

There was – and still is – an antique iron staircase clamped to the back of the building. It serves as a fire escape for both the upper floors. It was to this structure that the sergeant was referring.

'Yes, of course,' said Miss Earle. She led the sergeant across to the kitchen. He was greeted there by Thomas Anderson. Buckley scrutinised young Anderson's face.

Then looked closely at the woman's. Neither, as he was afterwards to testify, seemed to be in the least agitated.

'We saw a man climb over the wall at the end of the garden, didn't we Tom?' said Miss Earle. The lad nodded, 'Yes.'

Buckley made his way across the kitchen into the small adjoining scullery, stepped out on to the iron landing and, followed by Anderson, who had said that he would go down with him and show him where the man had scrambled over the wall, went carefully down the narrow stair. With Miss Earle watching from the head of the stair, the two men descended to the lower level, and, after a swift survey of the small yard, walked to the end of the little handkerchief of garden at the rear of the building, the police sergeant leading the way.

Thence they progressed, in investigative mode, to the next-door garden, that of Cambridge House – a diminutive splotch of green, surrounded by trees fully dressed in summer foliage, bordered by carefully tended, well-kept flower beds – which they minutely inspected. Beyond scratched bricks and torn Virginia creeper where the intruder had climbed over the wall, they found nothing. Somewhat deflated, they retraced their footsteps back to No. 17 territory, Sergeant Buckley coming to a stop midway to look over the garden wall.

As the young man carried on and drew closer to the building he heard a weird sound, as of irregular and heavy breathing coming from the pool of darkness at the foot of the iron staircase. He thought that it might be a dog. He wanted it to be a dog. Samuel Butcher, the occupant of the top flat, kept a dog, but he was away that weekend. Moving cautiously forward, Anderson stepped into the blackness, struck a match and was horrified to see, lying there before him, the body of a man. He lay supine under the iron staircase, partly on the scullery steps of the ground-floor flat, his feet pointing to the yard. Thomas Anderson did not know it at the time, but the dying man was his father, the actor Weldon Atherstone.

And he had been murdered.

It would have required a greater power of imagination than resided in young Tom Anderson to summon out of the prone and crumpled figure collapsed upon the ground the theatrically smart-suited, proud-bearinged, grease-painted, powdered and prinked player stepping, shining-shoed, on to the stage, into the limelight. No. He did not, in this broken, bloodstained object, recognise his father.

Tom called out to Buckley, 'Quick, there's a man lying here.'

The sergeant ran forward, bent over the man. 'Get me a light,' he said.

Miss Earle, who was standing on the iron stair landing outside her scullery door, heard the sergeant's request, and bore part way down the stair a small brass lamp with a single globe, which Anderson lit. By its light Buckley took one more look at the unconscious man, and very firmly told Miss Earle that if she was nervous she had better not come down any further. 'This man has been cut to pieces,' he said.

Meanwhile, Buckley asked Tom to go out to Noice, who was sitting with Glanville outside in Prince of Wales Road in his car, and ask him to fetch a doctor. Noice drove off and knocked up Dr Charles Ayton Marrett, general practitioner, of Clifton House, 58 Cambridge Road, Battersea Park.

On Noice's return Buckley asked him, 'Do you know this man? Have you seen him before?'

'No, I know nothing about him,' was the reply.

Having arranged the carrying of the injured man into the kitchen of the empty flat, Buckley sent for the divisional surgeon of police for V Division, Battersea – Dr Felix Charles Kempster, general practitioner, of 59 Battersea Bridge Road – and despatched Harold

Glanville to Battersea Police Station to inform the officer in charge of the situation.

It might, I think, be as well here to get the topography right. It is slightly complicated. No. 17 Prince of Wales Road (which is now Prince of Wales Drive) was, as we have already noted, also known as No. 8 Clifton Gardens. The next-door house, No. 19 Prince of Wales Road, was Cambridge House, which, in 1910, was a girls' school. It stood on the corner of Prince of Wales Road and Rosenau Road, which latter, at right angles to Prince of Wales Road, runs up to Petworth Street, and, if you then turn to the right, proceed to the end of Petworth Street, turn left into Albert Bridge Road and continue a very short distance north, you come to Albert Bridge and the river. The back garden of Cambridge House stretches down into Rosenau Road. Running along the sides at the rear, between Cambridge House (No. 19) and No. 17, there is a narrow, low-walled passageway or alley, a tradesman's route, accessed from Prince of Wales Road at the front, from which it is possible to enter the gardens of both premises.

Inspector Emmanuel Geake was taking the night parade at Battersea Police Station when, at about 9.45 p.m., Glanville arrived at the station. Hearing that a man had been shot at No. 17 Prince of Wales Road, and that a man had been seen running away, Geake promptly sent off telegrams to the divisional superintendent and to Divisional Inspector Edward Badcock. He also summoned Dr Kempster. Thereafter, he proceeded immediately to No. 17, taking with him a police ambulance and four constables, whom he posted at the front and back of the premises so that no one could leave, and to prevent any possible footprints in the back garden from interference.

He himself entered the front garden, jumped over a four-foot wall into the tradesmen's passage, which ran between No. 17 and No. 19, Cambridge House, and jumped back over the same wall into the rear garden of No. 17, where he saw Dr Marrett and Sergeant Buckley attending to the dying man. Then he went into the house and busied himself hunting for clues.

The first thing to seize his attention was a parcel on the mantelpiece in the kitchen of the empty ground-floor flat. It proved to be a pair of heavy brown boots, wrapped neatly up in brown paper. They had evidently belonged to the dead man, whose feet now bore red-and-blue-check felt carpet slippers.

Atherstone and a friend had been walking along the Waterloo Road on their way to a rehearsal for Fred Moule's *Grip of the Law* sketch when they saw a pair of red-and-blue-check slippers in the window of a shop. 'I must have a pair of those,' said Atherstone, and went in and purchased them.

It had been shortly after 9.45 p.m. that Dr Marrett had arrived at No. 17, to be joined there very soon by Dr Kempster. The two medical men had examined and assessed the injured Weldon Atherstone. The man was not dead, but deeply unconscious. He was lying on his back with his head turned to the left. They saw that he had been shot in the right-hand side of his face, just above the mouth. There was not much blood on the face and no grave disfigurement. However, on turning the head to the right, they discovered a second shot wound in the left temple, and the man's left eye was hanging out on the cheek. Both of the shot wounds were still bleeding. The doctors were unable to do anything to help him, and he died at 10.20 p.m. without regaining consciousness. Dr Kempster noted that the scullery steps on which he had previously been partially lying were covered with clotted blood. There had obviously been considerable haemorrhage.

At around half-past ten Detective-Sergeant Harry Purkiss searched the body of the deceased, and, the search completed, the body was taken to the Battersea mortuary.

In the course of his search Sergeant Purkiss had

discovered in one of the dead man's pockets a small red memorandum book, or kind of diary, tucked inside which was a visiting card reading,

> T. Weldon Atherstone
> Leading Character Actor
> 14 Great Percy Street, W.C.

This 'diary' proved to contain significant entries.

It was about 11 p.m. when Inspector Badcock arrived on the scene. He proceeded to find two pieces of a bullet in the downstairs scullery sink, and, eight feet away on the scullery floor, three pieces of a spectacle frame, together with some fragments of crushed glass.

He then went upstairs, interviewed Miss Earle and took the following statement from her:

I am a teacher of the Academy of Dramatic Art, Gower Street, and occupy 8B flat at Clifton Gardens, 17 Prince of Wales Road, Battersea. I have lived there and at the flat beneath for about eight years. Thomas Weldon Anderson lying dead, was an actor, whose stage name was Weldon Atherstone. He was married and lived at 14 Great Percy Street, King's Cross, in lodgings, having been separated from his wife before I knew him. He had four children, whose names I give: Constance C., Thomas Frederick, Doris Monica, William Gordon. I first met Mr Thomas Weldon Anderson when on a theatrical tour upwards of eight years ago, and have since been on intimate relations with him, and he has come and stayed with me when he likes.

About 8.30 or 8.45 tonight, the son, Thomas Frederick Anderson, called upon me by an appointment made on a postcard asking if he might call. I had known him from a boy and he has always visited me. I replied that he might call, and he did so. On his arrival about 8.40 p.m. we sat and talked in the front sitting-room until about nine.

Then I showed him some decorations that I had carried out in my bedroom, and then we went to take supper in the kitchen. While doing so we heard two shots in rapid succession, and going into the scullery adjoining, opened a door leading on to the back stairs. Looking out, we saw a man scrambling over the wall dividing our back from the adjoining one to the right of us. I wanted to go down to see what the matter was, but Anderson would not let me. We resumed our meal, thinking that someone might have fired to scare a thief. A few minutes later a knock came at the door, and I admitted Sergeant Buckley ... I saw Mr Thomas Weldon Anderson about seven weeks ago, when he called with his son, Thomas Frederick. They stayed to tea, and through the evening, and we were happy together. The time before that I saw Mr Thomas Weldon Anderson was about eight weeks ago. He called before I came home and I believe was let through the back by one of the other flats. He stayed with me that night but seemed sulky. At breakfast the next morning we quarrelled, because he said I had another man in the flat. I denied it. He then pointed to the sofa, and said that it was indented, and had been laid on. He struck me. I called for help. I went out and into the park. On my return he said, 'It is all over,' meaning our friendship. As he had been frequently jealous because I had my male pupils, I gave them up a year ago, and had got used to his jealousy.

After the quarrel he called in my absence, and left my latchkey with a note asking me to forward his letters to an address he had written, and this made me think he might not come again. My home was always open to him, and he knew it. I know of no one who had any feeling against him, and I had behaved like a mother to his boys, the eldest of whom I had taken great interest in, and had instructed ...

Dr Kempster, who went up to see Miss Earle, found her in what he described as a condition of extreme nervous collapse. She was trembling in every limb and complaining bitterly of the cold. Beads of perspiration were dropping from her face, which was ashen grey. She was almost pulseless and he ordered her to have brandy. He remained with her until 1.45 a.m.

At a few minutes after eleven, Inspector Geake was standing chatting outside the front door of the block of flats when suddenly young Anderson appeared. He said that he was feeling sick and needed some fresh air.

'Do you know a man named Atherton?' asked Geake, who happened to be holding the card from the memorandum book in his hand and had misread the name on it.

'No, but I know a man named Atherstone,' said Anderson.

Geake showed him the visiting card. 'That's my father's card,' he said.

'I'll have to ask you to come with me to the station,' was Geake's response.

Anderson protested fiercely. 'I *can't.*' He was worried about getting into his lodgings. 'I *must* be in at half-past eleven, otherwise I can't get in. I haven't a key. I'll be locked out. Can I go?'

But Geake was adamant: 'No. I'm sorry but you'll have to come to the station.'

When they got there the lad was shown the pair of brown boots from the kitchen mantelpiece at No. 17. He recognised them as his father's. He sat down on a bench and covered his face with his hands. 'Good God! Do you mean it was my father I found lying there!'

'I don't know,' replied the inspector.

'Has he got a false moustache on?' asked Anderson.

'No, he's clean-shaven,' came the reply.

Evidently, what Anderson had seen on the dead man's face and mistaken for a moustache had been a dark streak of blood.

Happening to encounter Sergeant Purkiss at the

station, Anderson asked him to describe the dead man to him.

Purkiss said, 'He's a man about my height, long, thin face, similar to your own, and clean-shaven.'

Young Anderson burst into tears. 'Good God! I have seen my father die.'

As daylight broke, Badcock and other officers examined the garden at the rear of Cambridge House. With the gathering light they were able to make out distinct impressions of feet, in Badcock's opinion a man's boots, size nine, which certainly did not match up with Atherstone's brown boots. The prints, inside and immediately under the Cambridge House garden boundary wall facing on to Rosenau Road, were going to and coming from the direction of No. 17. They were made by light boots with no nails on them. On the opposite side of the garden of Cambridge House there were a number of indistinct footmarks, leaves were broken off the bough of a tree, and there were other marks on the Virginia creeper around the trelliswork.

So to what conclusions did the physical evidence gleaned by these dawn-lit gardening excursions lead? Undoubtedly Atherstone's assailant entered the premises by the back. Distinct marks of both ingress and egress, and of someone struggling for a foothold on the Cambridge House garden wall, had been discovered. Marks had been observed, too, on the loose mould of the garden, betraying both a stealthy approach and a hurried return journey. There were deductions also to be made. For instance, had the intruder turned round, panic flooded, immediately after loosing the fatal shots, and scaled the proximate wall, he would have landed straight on to a glass roof in the adjoining garden of Cambridge House. His use of the same route for flight as that of his coming would seem to suggest knowledge of No. 19's garden prior to the enforced exit. He actually ran the full length of the garden, scrambled to the top of the wall, negotiated the adjoining tradesmen's passage, and clambered thence into the Cambridge House garden, from which he emerged over the wall on to the pavement of Rosenau Road.

As things turned out, the murderous visitant had not succeeded in preserving total invisibility. He had been seen by at least three eyewitnesses.

The first was Edward Noice. Walking home along Rosenau Road, on the opposite side to Cambridge House, at half-past nine that July evening, he heard the unmistakable sound of shots, seeming to come from the back of No. 17. He stood still, wondering what the shots meant. And, as he stood bewildered, he heard a strange sound which he afterwards realised had been that of splintering trelliswork. He looked across the road to the grounds of Cambridge House, and saw a man coming through the trees, pushing his way through the shrubs. Then, in a matter of split seconds, he saw the man appear on the top of the garden wall, roll over it as rapidly as he could, drop to the pavement and disappear at full tilt up Rosenau Road.

The second witness was Mrs Emma Lewis, a working housekeeper, of 24 Juer Street, Battersea. She, with a little girl of about five, was returning at around 9.30 p.m. along Rosenau Road from shopping in Battersea Park Road when she heard two shots fired in quick succession. On looking in the direction from which the sounds had come – that was the grounds of Cambridge House – she was startled to see a man in the act of springing on to the wall. He dropped to the pavement of Rosenau Road about a foot from where she was standing, and ran off as fast as his legs would carry him. Mrs Lewis had at first thought that he had come over the wall in search of assistance, but on second thoughts concluded that a crime had been committed.

The third witness was Arthur Jones, a salesman, who lived at 44A Isis Street, Earlsfield. He had been on his way home from work, and at 9.30 p.m., passing along Rosenau Road heading for Battersea Park Road, he heard two pistol shots and a man ran past him, breathing very hard. The man ran towards Petworth Street. Jones thought at the time that someone had committed suicide and that the man was running for a doctor.

What kind of a picture of this running man did the amalgam of these witnesses' recollections present? The triumvirate's testimony was disappointingly variant, yielding minimal useful consensus – no stamp of remarkability, no heartening perlustration to facilitate subsequent identification. Description is a corroborative functionary interchange, exportation of interpretative impression dependent upon individual percipience. Thus, Noice said that the only impression that he got of the man was that he was about five feet and six inches in height. He could not say how the man was dressed, only that he was not of the labouring type. He was not wearing an overcoat. He did not think that he held anything in his hands, as he had used both of them to help him get over the wall, which was about seven feet high. Noice said that he had never seen the man before. He also said that he saw Mrs Lewis in the road and she spoke to him afterwards.

Mrs Lewis put the man's height at about 5 feet and three inches, and she said that he was broad-shouldered. He was wearing a dark jacket suit, the back of the jacket of which she noticed was either dusty or muddy, and one of those bowler hats of the newest shape. He had nothing in his hands and wore no gloves. She was unable to say if he had any hair on his face, but she thought she could recognise him again in profile, or by his back. She did not hear him say anything. She carried away the overriding image of a soft, round, white moon face.

Arthur Jones, like Emma Lewis, had caught a passing glimpse of the man's face. He could not say if it had any hair on it or not, but if it had it was a fair moustache.

From the general effect of his dress one would sooner think the man a clerk than a labourer. He had on a tweed peaked cap. He seemed to be wearing light boots, as he made little noise in running. Although Jones had originally put the man's age as about twenty-five or twenty-six, he would subsequently revise his estimate to about twenty or thirty years.

A couple of further potential witnesses were traced – two boys who had been passing along Rosenau Road at the material time. They said that the man was between twenty-three and thirty, and stood five feet three inches.

The combined testimony of the eyewitnesses did not prove of much practical value, but what was useful was when, at 1 a.m., at Battersea Bridge Road Police Station, Noice, confronted with Thomas Frederick Anderson, stated, 'That is not the man who got over the wall. I'm positive.'

At 8.30 a.m. on Sunday 17 July, Detective Sergeant John Parker accompanied the Anderson brothers to the Battersea Mortuary, where they identified the body as that of their father, and William said that to the best of his belief the felt carpet slippers which the dead man had been wearing were the slippers which he had seen his father wearing at Great Percy Street on 2 July last.

The body of Thomas Weldon Anderson was removed on 21 July from the Battersea Mortuary to the undertaker's premises of Mr Henry Smith in Battersea Park Road. It was enclosed in an elm shell, which was placed in an oak coffin, bearing the inscription,

Thomas Weldon Anderson

Age 47

Died on July 16, 1910

On the morning of Friday 22 July, the cortège formed at the house of Thomas Weldon Anderson's sisters,

No. 62 Tufnell Park Road. The mourners rode in two broughams drawn by bay horses. The interment was to take place in Abney Park Cemetery, Stoke Newington. There were very few people at the cemetery. Neither Anderson's widow, who was living in Ireland and wrote a 'very womanly' letter of sympathy to her sisters-in-law, nor Elizabeth Earle was present. Thomas Lightfoot Weldon was not there either. There were some beautiful wreaths, including a very large one from the children. The chief mourner was Anderson's son, Tom, accompanied by his brother and two sisters. By his special desire, Tom helped to carry the coffin from the hearse to the family grave. The interment took place at midday. The service was conducted by the Reverend A. Palmer.

'I have no idea why anyone should take my father's life, or why anyone should feel enmity towards him,' Tom Anderson told a press interviewer:

He was of a lovable nature, kind and sympathetic, and I should say the last in the world to make an enemy. He made friends everywhere. We had known Miss Earle and her late mother for a very long time, and the friendship was continued after her mother's death. Let me tell you exactly what was the position also as between my father and myself. He had not the slightest objection to my visiting her, in fact we often went together. Nor was there the slightest secrecy as to the visits we paid. He knew I was going there on Saturday, although I did not expect that he would meet me there. But it would not have surprised me in the least to see his face at the door at any moment. As to his taking off his boots and putting on slippers in the bottom flat, I can only say that I cannot understand his motive. But I would rather not discuss points of that kind, because the police have warned me not to talk about what took place, and I do not want to interfere with their efforts to find the murderer.

As the *Dundee Courier* observed, 'Should an arrest and investigation follow, it is probable that a story of love, hatred, or revenge will be unfolded exceeding in dramatic intensity any real life tragedy of recent times.'

Part Five
Murder Solved and Unsolved

7

Manhunt

The violent death of Weldon Atherstone – the Battersea Flat Mystery, as it became known – set a pretty dish of puzzlement before the police. Their first theory was that the shooting was the result of an unexpected random encounter between the actor and a burglar. Police and press both set to work most vigorously to discover the facts which lay behind the tragedy.

The headmistress of the Cambridge House High School for Girls, which adjoined the Prince of Wales Road flats, told a representative of the press that on the Saturday evening she had been having her supper when she was suddenly startled by the noise of two loud shots fired in rapid succession coming from the next-door back garden. For a moment or two she had been too terrified to move. When she did so, she found Rosenau Road filled with a crowd of anxious people.

The *London Evening News* of Monday 18 July summed up the situation very fairly: 'With only a slight and almost useless description of the suspected murderer, the police have another difficult crime problem in front of them.'

By the following day – 19 July – a few personal details were beginning to emerge. Mr Lilford Arthur of Denton's Theatrical Agency in Maiden Lane told the press:

Mr Atherstone has been known at this agency for two or three years, and an examination of the books reveals the fact that, while he was living at the time of his murder in Great Percy Street, King's Cross, his previous address was Prince of Wales Road, Battersea, where he was shot. He must, therefore, have been well known in that neighbourhood, and not merely a stranger or even as a casual visitor to the friend of the family, Miss Earle, who also lives there, and to whom his son was paying a visit at the very time of the tragedy.

Commented the *Pall Mall Gazette*: 'To Mr Arthur the statement that Mr Atherstone carried a life-preserver came entirely as a surprise. He spoke of him as a very quiet man, and the last person in the world whom he would have supposed to have any need to go about so armed. Only last week he called once or twice at the office of the agency, and on one of these occasions he was accompanied by his son.'

A well-known actor and old friend of both the Atherstone family and Miss Earle told a *Daily Mail* representative:

I have known Atherstone for the past twenty years [i.e. since 1890]. I played with him ten years ago and knew him as a strong and capable actor. He and his boys have been frequent visitors at my house. Miss Earle, who is a friend of mine and my wife's, has been here often. For some fifteen years, and until quite recently, Atherstone lived with the Earles – Mrs Earle, her son and daughter. And then, after the death of Mrs Earle, about four years ago [i.e. 1906], Mrs Earle's son [John Lloyd] went to Australia three years ago [i.e. 1907]. About two years ago [i.e. 1908] Atherstone moved to 14 Great Percy Street in order to be near his sons.

The *Star* reported that in the course of an interview Mr G. W. Ryder, the veteran actor, recalled:

I knew Weldon Atherstone very well indeed, and he was one of the nicest men I ever met. Something like five years ago [i.e. 1905], he was acting heavy lead with my daughter in a play called *The Temptress*. Previously he had played a leading part in *Under the Red Cross*. But his greatest part, and that in which he achieved much success, was that of the Duke of Gloucester in *Jane Shore*. He was said to be one of the best impersonators in that part that has been seen on the stage. About this time last year [i.e. March 1909] he was at the Shakespeare, Clapham Junction, in a play called *Revenge*.

20 July

By this time the newspapers (*Evening News*) are announcing that 'not the slightest belief now remains that the Battersea murderer was a burglar. The theory is accepted that Mr Atherstone was in the back garden under Miss Earle's flat on some errand that arose from jealousy.'

The *Star* states that

the police are certain of their information on the following points:

1. The crime was not committed by a burglar, but by a man who knew well the flat and the neighbourhood.

2. Mr Anderson saw the murderer lurking in the back garden when he was about to ascend the spiral iron staircase. He challenged him and the murderer fired. The murdered actor and his murderer knew each other. The first shot went through the actor's cheeks and entered the scullery window of the bottom (empty) flat.

3. There followed a terrific struggle. There are signs that the actor's assailant clawed him down the face with his left hand, and, firing a second shot at close quarters, blew out Mr Anderson's right eye.

With these facts in their knowledge the police are still a

long way from discovering who was the actual murderer. In the meantime the following questions are being asked:

Who was the murderer?

Why did he murder Mr Anderson?

What was the motive that brought an armed man to the back garden?

Was he an individual cherishing some private grudge against Anderson?

If he was, did he track Anderson down to Clifton Gardens that Saturday night? Did he go there *intending* to shoot Anderson? Or only armed in case of emergency?

Why was Anderson at Battersea at all?

Why had he taken off his boots and put on carpet slippers?

Was it that he might move about noiselessly?

If so, why?

Deceased was said to have left his Great Percy Street lodgings only an hour before the tragedy took place.

Less than a month ago [i.e. *c.* June 1910] he played in a sketch called *The Grip of the Law* at the Battersea Empire. In the course of his part he was supposed to throw the villain into a cauldron [used for bacon-curing], and his final exclamation in the sketch was 'Thank God, my father's death has been avenged.'

Mr Fred Moule describes Atherstone as a very intellectual man and one who during the past fifteen years has seen many ups and downs'.

21 July

Shortly after Wednesday midnight (reports the *Daily Mail* of Friday 22 July), Miss Earle fell into a state of collapse. She sank on to a couch and was unable to recognise or speak to the two women who were in the house. A hasty message was at once sent to Dr

Macrory, who after an examination said that Miss Earle was prostrate through shock and would not be able to reply to any interrogations for several days. This fact was communicated to Divisional Detective Inspector Badcock when he called at the house. Miss Earle's friends said, 'The doctor has strictly forbidden anyone – even the police – to be admitted to Miss Earle. She is still in a state of complete collapse and can scarcely speak.'

The illness of Miss Earle naturally hinders to a great extent the investigations by the police. Miss Earle's long acquaintance with Anderson, who had lodged for many years with her mother and herself, led to the hope that she would be able to recall some incident or name that might aid the police to solve the mystery.

So evident is it that there was a struggle between Anderson and his assailant that it is now considered possible that the murderer's clothes were stained with the blood of his victim. The bullets used were of .320 calibre – a common size for revolvers. The fact that the bullet which struck the side of the scullery door did not lodge in the woodwork, but dropped into the sink, shows that either the weapon used was of a very cheap pattern or that the cartridge had a very weak explosive charge.

Some hundreds of [Anderson's] letters have come into the possession of the police. They have an important bearing on the mystery of his stealthy visit to the flat on Saturday armed with a life preserver. The theory that he had intended to try to catch a burglar has now been discarded by the police.

The caretaker at the Prince of Wales Road flats yesterday stated that she saw a man who, she believes, was Anderson, apparently watching the flats from the opposite side of the road a fortnight ago.

A curious fact was recalled by a friend of Anderson's yesterday. Anderson, he said, was discussing, in his presence, crime mysteries with Miss Earle, some months ago, and began to exercise his wits in an endeavour to imagine a crime, apparently baffling, which would be capable of a very simple explanation. He wrote imaginary newspaper headlines and read them aloud with much satisfaction.

22 July

Nearly a week gone by. Observed the *Daily Chronicle*: 'The Battersea murder becomes the more puzzling as the days pass and nothing is discovered as to the motive or person of the murderer.'

Failing to trace anyone with personal animosity against the dead man, the police resorted to the formulation of a most complex motivational theory of their own. It was that three men were directly or indirectly concerned in the tragedy, and that Miss Earle was the innocent cause of a passionate feud which had arisen between two of these men. According to this theory, Atherstone had somehow learned that a person known to him intended to be at Miss Earle's flat that July Saturday night – for what purpose Atherstone may have formed a mistaken judgment. He knew that his son, Thomas, was to be at Miss Earle's that same evening, and he may have suspected that the third man proposed to be there to spy on Tom, or, possibly, to attack him. Determining to teach the putative intruder a lesson, Atherstone made his way to the empty flat to await there the coming of the man whom he regarded as a spy, as a blackguard, or both. Apparently, the intruder had also somehow learned that Atherstone intended to be present and got there first. He was lying in wait in the backyard when Atherstone, blissfully unaware of the other man's presence, stepped forth into the rapidly deepening darkness. What then happened, when it is assumed that both men were armed and determined to fight, was inevitable.

That Friday (22 July) the coroner John Troutbeck was

in Battersea, apparently studying the case. In any event Mr Troutbeck was seen taking away with him when he left the Battersea Coroner's Court on the Friday afternoon a large number of closely typewritten sheets. The content of these were the statements that had been taken by Detective Inspector Badcock and his subordinates. The case absorbed all Troutbeck's attention. During a journey by car from Battersea to Vauxhall, he perused the papers with evident care and was oblivious of all else. When, having arrived at his journey's end, he folded the papers up, his features indicated deep perplexity.

In the absence of any solid information, speculation was, of course, rife. The *Dundee Courier* of 23 July reported, factually, that the police had received very valuable information from Mr Fred Moule, an author and producer of playlets.

Mr Moule made the following statement:

On 21 May last I wrote to Anderson giving him an engagement to play in *In the Grip of the Law,* and forwarding the words of the part he had to play. This letter was sent to 17 Prince of Wales Road, and in it I asked him to meet me in Bedford Street, Strand, at 1 p.m. on Monday, 23 May. At 2 p.m. he turned up, and expressed surprise at the idea of an appointment. I told him I had written to Prince of Wales Road. He said, 'That explains it; I have not been home all night.' He said then he would go and fetch the letter and the part, but explained he was leaving his lodgings there and would in future live at 14 Great Percy Street, King's Cross. On Wednesday (25 May) or the Thursday (26 May) following, after a rehearsal, he told me why he had left Prince of Wales Road. He was jealous – of whom or on account of whom he did not say. He added that he felt very keenly the parting with an old friend of his family and charming lady in whose flat he had lodged for many years. He spoke of her as an intellectual companion, one who sympathized with him in his love of books and could talk to him. He mentioned no one by name, but he was clearly very upset about the affair and the cause of the breaking of this friendship. Starting on the following Monday, 30 May, at Bow Palace he played with me at Sadler's Wells, the Foresters, the Battersea Palace, and at the Surrey Theatre, finishing on 2 July. While we were at the Battersea Palace I said – 'It's a pity you don't live at Prince of Wales Road still. You would not have so far to go home.' He replied: 'It's finished. That will never be opened up again.' I had no part for him in my next sketch, *Gretna Green*. On Wednesday last (13 July) I saw him for a few minutes in the Strand. On Friday night (the night before the murder) he came up to the Sadler's Wells and spent the night with me. His younger son was with him. We parted at midnight. He was cheerful but a little excited, and he described dramatically for me some parts of *Alias Jimmy Valentine*, the burglar play which he had been at a few nights before. It was unusual for him to act like that in public.

Mr Moule's circumstantial account of the reason why Anderson left Miss Earle's flat in which he had lodged for so many years is corroborated in several quarters. There can be no doubt that Anderson became moody. On three occasions – twelve months ago last Christmas [i.e. 1909] and on 22 May 1910 – it is alleged that he struck the lady with whom he lodged. It is also alleged that he refused to allow her to teach elocution to any but women pupils. Those who have followed most closely the intricacies of this mystery are now convinced that Anderson's reason was obsessed by one of those fits of passion when he took his carpet slippers and his piece of cable to the empty flat beneath the one in which he formerly lived. It is true that he knew his son was above, but in another quarter of an hour the son would have gone. And he could then quietly steal up the steps outside the flat and enter the flat he knew so well. If Anderson went to Prince of Wales Road with this murderous intent the rest of the mystery explains itself without difficulty. His intention known – it is alleged that he was observed in the neighbourhood several times during the previous fortnight and his son has suggested that he was there on Wednesday (13th) night of last week – it is not difficult to imagine a silent watcher, who, seeing him enter the empty flat, jumped over the garden wall and lay in wait for him at the foot of the staircase.

24 July

'Our London Letter' in the *Herts. And Cambs. Reporter* carried the subheading 'Stranger than Fiction' and the information that 'the Battersea murder is even more mystifying than anything to be found in the pages of a six-shilling novel. After nearly a fortnight of active inquiry and search the police have made no arrest.'

The *Umpire* announced the discovery of a scented left-hand glove stained with nicotine about the fingers. A minor mystery in itself. Nothing more was ever heard of it.

29 July

Lloyds Weekly News, referring to the entry in Atherstone's red diary, comes up with the question, 'Who was "B"?' and talks of 'mysterious references to "B"', adding that 'the answer to this question may provide the solution of the problem, "Who killed Thomas Weldon Atherstone?"' The report goes on to explain,

At the inquest … the police produced a diminutive red leather memorandum book, in which the dead man had kept a kind of diary. On one side were details under the initials 'W.A.', which evidently refers to himself; on the other were memoranda under the initial 'B'. The contents of the diary were kept secret at the request of the police, who, however, made the significant statement that they suggested that the contents of the book indicated that the dead man was jealous of Miss Earl [*sic*]. Was 'B' the man who provoked the jealousy? And who and where is 'B'? [I can provide the answer. 'B' stands for 'Bessie', which is the name by which Atherstone called Elizabeth Earle.]

31 July
The People stated that it was now in a position to publish certain extracts from the diary of the dead man which showed how deep-rooted was his jealousy. 'Certain entries which it is not advisable to publish show that he had been watching Miss Earle's flat for some months past in the expectation of meeting a visitor, and others show that he was fast losing his reason. No sane man would write such statements, even in a private pocketbook.'

Two entries dated about the middle of July show how the murdered man watched the house, and how he acted as an amateur detective in his endeavour to find out who was the man he imagined to be paying attentions to Miss Earle.

ENTRY NO. 1 Watched the house until 11.30 when lights were turned out.
ENTRY NO. 2 Found bunch of flowers in the ash bin.

The dead man argued in his diary that someone had evidently made Miss Earle a present of the flowers, a conclusion which she denied.

What was perceived as perhaps the most significant of all the entries in the diary runs, 'If he had kept away from her, if he had broken from the spell of her fascination and remained out of reach, this would never have happened. He has no one to blame but himself. We all reap as we have sown.'

In addition to the extracts quoted above, there are

a number of other effusions on the subjects of love and friendship written in the diary. For instance, a comparison of love with friendship affirms, 'Friendship is but a substitute for love, and cannot exist beside it, unless the lover and friend be one and the same person. They suppose that a man can love a woman with the best kind of love, and may have at the same time a friend with whom he is in entire sympathy. Why not? Because he cannot serve two masters – either his friendship or his love must be imperfect.'

Many of the extracts would seem to be entries from other books. For example: 'Love is complete, and being so demands the whole, and is not satisfied with less than the whole, any more than it is satisfied with giving less than it has.' And 'The prime essence of love is that it should be complete, making no reservation, and allowing of no check from the reason. When the heart gets the mastery it knows neither rest nor mercy. If the heart is good the result will be good; if bad, evil.'

'Certain of the notes scribbled in his diary by the murdered actor are of too personal a character for production here,' says *The People*. They continue:

> Every item of the daily life of Miss Earle that came to his notice is entered and commented on in such a manner that the police could only conclude that he was fast going out of his mind. They had at first hoped that they would find in the diary some clue as to the name of the man whom the deceased hoped to meet at Miss Earle's flat on the fatal night; but so many names were mentioned that it was of little use. One man against whom deceased's suspicions seem to have been greatest, is now on tour in America, while most of the others referred to are in the provinces. Nevertheless, each possible clue is being most carefully sifted, and even now the police have not lost all hope that an arrest may be made in the near future. They have had several other interviews with both Miss

Earle and the murdered man's son, but the state of health of the former militates against the police. Miss Earle is about to undergo an operation, and upon her recovery she intends leaving the country and going to Australia, where her brother resides. Her departure, however, will not take place until the inquest on her one-time lover has been concluded.

1 August

The mystery surrounding the death of Mr Weldon Atherstone remains as deep as ever. The local police say they are still far from solving the problem. Investigations are being made in every direction, and particularly with regard to the names found in the murdered man's diary, but, as yet, nothing has been discovered which would justify the police in taking any action. They express themselves as being without the faintest clue as to the identity of the man who was seen to jump over the garden wall close to the scene of the tragedy.

4 August

A new development is reported. Information is stated to have reached the police from an acquaintance of the murdered actor, which, it is hoped, may lead up to a tangible clue, announces the *Dundee Courier*:

> The pivot of the case is the answer to the question – Whose was the revolver? If, as it seems now more than probable, it belonged to Anderson, the unseen struggle in the garden is presented in an entirely new aspect. There undoubtedly was a struggle, which in all probability was still proceeding when the shots were fired. The conviction is forced upon the police that the crime was committed ... by someone who was well acquainted with the parties. The man may have set out in the first instance on the mission of peace-maker. Who the rival is who is referred to in the dead man's diary has yet to be ascertained. An

extract seems to suggest the man, whoever he was, had undertaken to give up visiting Miss Earle, but had not fulfilled that promise. The entry is dated 14 July, two days before the crime.

The article goes on to quote the 'watched house until 11.30' and 'flowers in ash bin' entries, already quoted, and repeats the 'if he had ... remained out of reach, this would never have happened' and states, 'The phrase "out of reach" is specially significant in the light of after events.'

5 August

According to *The South Western Star*, during the week rumours had been set about that certain clues had been found which would be likely to lead to the identification of the man who had shot Atherstone, but ...

From enquiries made by our representative in a reliable quarter, it appears that the supposed clues are quite insubstantial. On Wednesday [3 August] it was reported and published that the police, in the course of their enquiries, came across a lady residing in the vicinity of Clifton Gardens who had been, it was stated, very much concerned about a leakage in the roof of her house. She was said to declare it was not there before the tragedy occurred. A day or two later she found that water was trickling through the slates. In an instant a new theory in connection with the murder was evolved – that after shooting Mr Anderson the murderer threw the revolver on the roof, and it fell heavily on the slates, breaking or dislodging them, and so causing the leakage. To use the words of one who knows, this theory is 'a load of swank', 'It would be practically impossible for a man to throw the revolver on the roof of any of the flats, especially in the dark. Even if such a feat was accomplished it is a hundred to one that the weapon would have dropped over the gutter into the garden, as the roofs slant at a very sharp angle. Up to the present the builder who has mended the slates has found no traces of a revolver either in the guttering or between the roof and the rafters. There is no doubt that the slates were dislodged by heavy rains during the storms.'

If the revolver could be found it would prove of great assistance to the investigators. There is a belief that it might have been thrown over the Albert Bridge into the river, and it is suggested that efforts should be made to discover it. Probably it is a very small weapon. The bullets fired from it were said to be not much larger in circumference than air-gun pellets.

An actor at a seaside resort has been interviewed at some length by a detective, who was unable to glean any fresh information.

At the end of last week we were informed that Miss Earle was preparing to go to Normandy until the inquest is resumed ... She had partially recovered from the shock received on the eventful night. And it is hoped that the change of air will completely restore her to her proper health.

12 August
An alien note of optimism.

There is just a possibility that a solution to the mystery ... will be forthcoming during the next few days. The police have arrested, upon another charge, a man who is said to bear a striking resemblance to the person seen running away by Noice and by those other witnesses.

Mrs Lewis has been shown a photograph of the man now in custody. 'It is a very similar face,' she said. 'Of course I only had a very imperfect look at him, and the light from the lamp was not very good. But that photograph is certainly not unlike him, and he looks about the same age.'

The man who is under arrest is known to be of

violent disposition. His description, which is only approximate, is: Age about 30, clean shaven, about 5 ft. 6 in. high, appears to belong to the clerical section of the wage-earning class, gives the impression of being a man of powerful build. In all particulars he resembles the man seen running away on the night of the murder.

The police have traced two more people who state that they saw the alleged murderer climb over the wall of the garden of the school next door and run down Rosenau Road. There has been some doubt on this point owing to the fact that several people who were in the neighbourhood did not notice any man climb over the wall.

These two new witnesses are young men of the middle-class and are of respectable character. They state that they heard two revolver shots, and shortly afterwards saw the figure of a man climbing over a 7-foot wall. Owing to the darkness they were unable to give any more detailed description than had been furnished by previous witnesses, but, so far as they go, the descriptions tally. The man they saw was below the average height, being less than 5 ft. 6 in. tall, and from 20 to 30 years of age. He was fairly well dressed.

Up to the present, no weapon has been found, though every imaginable place has been searched for the purpose. The finding of the revolver would be a valuable clue to the identity of the culprit.

The people mentioned in the actor's diary have been interviewed, but have given satisfactory accounts of their whereabouts on the day of the murder, and similar explanations have been given by other friends of the deceased actor.

Thomas Frederick Anderson told a press representative: 'Whatever happened, I am convinced my father was in the right and the man who attacked him was a coward. It has been suggested that the revolver may have been my father's. I do not believe it for a minute. He was not that sort of man. He was a man who would not make use of a weapon unless it was forced upon him. It is possible he has used a revolver in plays, but in private life I have never seen him with firearms. The fact that soft-nosed bullets were used shows a cruel intent on the part of the murderer. It is true that my father had armed himself with a piece of cable. But as it remained in his pocket it is clear he had no time to defend himself with it. This part of the affair, I assure you, is a mystery to me. I do not believe that my father was jealous of Miss Earle, in spite of the diary. I do not want to say much about that, but I should like to say this, that some of the entries are things which my father copied from books. The passage which has been reproduced in the papers ('If he had broken from the spell of her fascination,' etc.) is a quotation. It was my father's habit to jot down things in that way, for use, I suppose, on the stage. The language is not his at all.'

Young Mr Anderson admitted that the words 'Watched the house', suggested an act on his father's part, but if he was spying on Miss Earle's flat, his son could suggest no reason for it. 'The whole thing looks simple, and yet the more you examine it the more difficult it is to understand it,' he confessed. 'No attempts seem to have been made to follow the man who was running away. If only I had known! A good deal has been said about my not recognising my father when I first saw the body. It is true I was holding the light close to his face, but I kept my own head averted, I could not look at him and see him dying slowly with us unable to help him. I only took one glance, and the man, wounded as he was, appeared to have a moustache. Now my father was clean-shaven. Besides, my father was the last person I expected to see there. Even in the police station I did not realise at first who it was. When I looked at the body afterwards I should have had a difficulty in recognising my father had I not been sure then who it was. I can recall no one answering to the description of the man seen running away. I keep on thinking, thinking, but I can get no further.'

Mr William Anderson, the younger son, said he could form no theory to account for the murder.

'Upon inquiry last night we were informed that no further developments had taken place. The police are reticent, but we understand that they are by no means satisfied that the man in custody will turn out to be the 'wanted' person. The fresh door opened has, however, awakened a new interest in the case, and hundreds of people who passed the scene of the crime yesterday stood and observed the house.'

13 August

After a search extending over two continents all possible clues afforded by the mention of certain names in Weldon Atherstone's diary have been exhausted. 'The last of the men mentioned was located yesterday,' reveals the *Daily Mail*, 'and it was ascertained that he could not have had any connection with the crime, nor could he be expected to throw any light upon the circumstances leading up to it.'

26 August

A young man named Albert Bradshaw confessed to the Chatham Police that it was he who murdered Mr Anderson, the actor, at Battersea. A detective was sent from London. After questioning Bradshaw for some time, he came to the conclusion that the self-accuser was a victim of hallucination. Possibly the man was psychotic, and suffering from delusions and other symptoms, but it is considerably more likely that he was exhibiting the recognised 'compulsion to confess' which tends to show in disordered, inadequate individuals, sometimes in association with an hysterical need for attention, if indeed he was not deliberately concocting the story for the sake of notoriety. His further story that he was a deserter from the Navy proving false, the Chatham Magistrates discharged him.

8

The North London Cellar Murder

The long arm of coincidence flexed itself classically in January 1907. It was the time when bad feeling over pay and conditions manifest between the aggrieved Variety Artistes' Federation and the unyielding music-hall managers climaxed in the Music Hall Strike.

One artiste, Belle Elmore, was happy to seize the opportunity afforded her by the strike. She was engaged for a week at the Bedford Music Hall and at the Euston Palace of Varieties, but, as she stepped confidently forward to sing on the stage of the Euston, she had barely opened her mouth when a storm of hisses, catcalls and whistles greeted her honest endeavour. There were evidently those in the audience who regarded her as a 'blackleg', and her eager soprano as an infliction.

Deeply distressed, the weeping performer staggered back into the wings. Nobly, there stepped forward to comfort her the leading actor in a sketch that was to be played at the hall that night. He was extremely indignant at the treatment the muted lady singer had received, and expressed his sympathy with so obvious a sincerity that he succeeded in greatly consoling her.

The lady in distress was, in offstage life, Mrs Crippen. Her comforter was Weldon Atherstone, who was himself to suffer a similar reception from the audience that evening. Within a trio of years both would be dead, both sensationally murdered.

*

A certain medical gentleman by the name of Crippen and his secretary-typist, the self-styled Ethel Le Neve, playing in the true-life drama of the North London Cellar Murder, were enthralling the Metropolis and indisputably upstaging the South London Murder – the Battersea Flat Mystery.

Criminologically speaking, the year 1910 is indelibly stamped with the name Crippen. The interest in the Battersea mystery murder paled beside the compulsive fascination of the romantic runaway lovers, the vanished-into-thin-air Crippen and Le Neve.

The affair began quietly and inconspicuously enough. On 30 June 1910, Superintendent Frank Froest at New Scotland Yard received a visit from two of his friends: John Nash, a theatrical manager, and his wife Lillian, a music-hall artiste professionally known as Lil Hawthorne. They were worried. Returning home to London from an American tour, they had heard that their friend Cora Crippen was dead. She had, they were told, suddenly gone off to the States without a word of goodbye to anyone. Then, about five months ago, a notice had appeared in *The Era* announcing her death from pneumonia in California.

Cora's stage name had been Belle Elmore, but her career as a music-hall artiste had never been as successful as she had hoped. Her singing talent was of a markedly limited order. Realising at last that her dream of theatrical stardom was just that, but, anxious to retain an association with the stage and its folk, Cora had joined the Music Hall Ladies' Guild, a charitable body which had been founded in the autumn of 1906 to support the women and children of members of the profession who had fallen upon hard times. Cora became the Guild's honorary treasurer, and her friend, Lottie Albert, believed that this satisfactorily fulfilled her ambition to be connected with the theatre and stifled the disappointment of her failure to achieve distinction on the boards.

The Nashes had been to see the widowed Dr Crippen. He had told them that Cora had gone over to America on family business on 2 February, and died there on 23 March. Mrs Nash had felt something about him that she did not like – possibly distaste at his going about openly with his young typist, Ethel Le Neve, so soon after his wife's death.

Uneasy, too, were another couple of Cora's friends, Paul Martinetti, a retired star of the halls, and his wife Clara. They had been invited to dinner and whist at the Crippens' on the night of 31 January and bade farewell to their hosts at about 1.30 a.m. Neither they, nor anyone else, ever saw Cora alive again.

After listening to the Nashes' story, Froest summoned Chief Detective Inspector Walter Dew to his office, and it was decided that he should make discreet inquiries regarding the whereabouts of Cora Crippen, and that the best thing that he could do would be to interview her husband, Dr Crippen.

A week later, around ten o'clock on the morning of 8 July, accompanied by Detective Sergeant Arthur Mitchell, Dew, making an unannounced visit, arrived at the door of the Crippens' residence, 39 Hilldrop Crescent, Holloway, a large, semi-detached house standing well back from the road, behind a screen of overgrown trees. His ring was answered by Valentine Lecocq, a seventeen-year-old French girl, employed by Crippen as a servant since 11 June.

A neatly dressed young woman appeared, saying that she was Crippen's housekeeper, but Dew had spotted at once that she was wearing a diamond brooch, which, from the description he had been given, he suspected had once been the property of Mrs Crippen. 'You are Miss Le Neve, are you not?' he said. Flushing slightly, she replied, 'Yes, that's right.'

It turned out that the doctor had already left the house, so Drew and Mitchell, together with Ethel Le Neve, made their way to Albion House, a large block of flats on New Oxford Street where, on the third floor, Crippen had his office, and where the Guild met every Wednesday.

Dew found Crippen disarmingly straightforward.

'I suppose I had better tell the truth,' he said. 'The stories I have told about her death are untrue. As far as I know she is still alive.'

He said that during the last five years of their life together at Hilldrop Crescent there were frequent quarrels and that Cora got into the most violent tempers, and often threatened to leave him. The final incident came on the night of 10 January, when Mr and Mrs Martinetti were the Crippens' house guests:

On the Monday night, the day before I wrote the letter to the Guild resigning her position as treasurer, Mr and Mrs Paul Martinetti came to our place to dinner, and during the evening Mr Martinetti wanted to go to the lavatory. As he had been to our home several times, I did not take the trouble to go and show him where it was. After they had left my wife blamed me for not taking him to the lavatory, and abused me, and said: 'This is the finish of it. I won't stand it any longer. I shall leave you tomorrow, and you will never hear of me again.' She had said this so often that I did not take much notice of it, but she did say one thing that she had never said before: that I was to cover up any scandal with our mutual friends and the Guild the best way I could. Before this, she had told me frequently that the man she would go to was better able to support her than I was.

I came to business the next morning, and when I went home between five and six p.m. I found she had gone. ... I sat down to think it over as to how to cover up her absence without any scandal. I think the same night, or the next morning (Wednesday) I wrote a letter to the Guild saying she had gone away, which I also told several people. I afterwards realised that this would not be a sufficient explanation for her not coming back, and later on I told people that she was ill with bronchitis and pneumonia, and afterwards I told them she was dead from the ailment. I told them she was dead in California, but I have no recollection of telling anyone exactly where she died.

I then put an advertisement in *The Era* that she was dead, as I thought that would prevent people asking a lot of questions. Whatever I have said to other people in regard to her death is absolutely wrong, and I am giving this as an explanation. It is not true that she went away on legal business for me, or to see any relations in America. I did not receive any cables to say that she was ill, and it is not true that she was cremated at San Francisco, and that the ashes were sent to me, or that she sailed from Havre.

Crippen said that he and Cora had a joint account in the Charing Cross Bank, subject to the signature of either. It pleased her to think she was signing cheques, and she did so, and several blank cheques were always already signed by her and

some of them signed by me since her departure, and there is one here now (produced).

When my wife went away I cannot say whether she took anything with her or not, but I believe there is a theatrical travelling basket missing. She took some of her jewellery, I know, with her, but she left four rings behind, also a diamond brooch.

It is true that I was at the Benevolent Fund dinner at the Criterion with Miss Le Neve, and she wore the brooch my wife left behind. She has also worn my wife's furs ... and she is now living with me as my wife at Hilldrop Crescent. I have been intimate with her during the past three years. This is all I can tell you ...

Crippen had also spoken frankly about a man named Bruce Miller:

Cora told me that this man visited her, had taken her about, and was very fond of her, also she was fond of him. I must say that when she came to England from America her manner towards me was entirely changed, and she had cultivated a most ungovernable temper, and seemed to think I was not good enough for her, and boasted of the men of good position travelling on the boat who had made a fuss of her, and, indeed, some of these visited her at South Crescent [the street off Tottenham Court Road, where the Crippens lived before moving to Hilldrop Crescent], but I do not know their names.

I never saw the man Bruce Miller, but he used to call when I was out, and used to take her out in the evenings. It is quite four years since she ever went out at all to sing [i.e. 1906], and although we apparently lived very happily together, as a matter of fact there were very frequent occasions when she got into most violent tempers, and often threatened she would leave me, saying she had a man she could go to, and she would end it all. I have seen letters from Bruce to her, which ended 'with love and kisses to Brown Eyes'. About four years ago, in consequence of these frequent outbursts, I discontinued sleeping with her, and have never cohabited with her since. I never interfered with her movements in any way; she went in and out just as she liked, and did what she liked, it was of no interest to me. As I say, she frequently threatened to leave me, and said that if she did she would go right out of my life, and I should never see or hear from her again.

Crippen's replies had come freely. There had been no hesitation. His manner was that of a much maligned man eager only to clear the matter up by telling the whole truth. Dew was impressed by the man's demeanour. It was impossible to be otherwise. His very frankness was misleading. By admitting things which men normally like to hide, he gave the impression that he was telling the entire truth and had nothing to hide. He confessed, for instance, that his association with Le Neve had begun long before Mrs Crippen disappeared.

Dew then invited Ethel Le Neve to tell him all she knew.

She told him:

Since the latter end of February I have been living at 39 Hilldrop Crescent with Dr Crippen as his wife. I have been on intimate terms with Dr Crippen for between two and three years, but I have known him for ten years. I made his acquaintance by being in the same employ as he. I knew Mrs Crippen, and have visited at Hilldrop Crescent. She treated me as a friend. In the early part of February I received a note from Dr Crippen, saying Mrs Crippen had gone to America. About a week after he told me she had gone to America, I went to Hilldrop Crescent to put the place straight, as there were no servants kept; but at night I went to my lodgings. I did this daily for about a fortnight. The place appeared to be quite all right and quite as usual. He took me to the Benevolent Fund Dinner, and lent me a brooch to wear. Later on, he told me I could keep it. Afterwards he told me his wife was dead. I was very much astonished, but do not think I said anything to him about it. He gave me some furs of his wife's to wear, and I have been living with him ever since as his wife. My father and mother do not know what

I am doing, and think I am a housekeeper at Hilldrop
Crescent.

After writing down these statements, Dew, Mitchell,
Crippen and Le Neve took a 'growler' out to Holloway.
There, Dew and Mitchell entered each one of No. 39's eight
rooms in turn, systematically searching the wardrobes,
dressing tables, cupboards and every other likely nook and
cranny. Crippen and Le Neve escorted them throughout,
the little doctor seeming positively eager to help.

Belle Elmore's passion for clothes was inescapably
evident. There was the most extraordinary assortment
of women's finery in the bedrooms, in quantity enough
to fill a large van to overflowing, and a sufficiency of
ostrich feathers to furnish covering for Owen's *Dinornis
maximus* from beak to rump tip!

There were two rooms in the basement, or garden
floor – a breakfast room, its grubby net curtains
screening without a clustered Victorian green fernery,
and the kitchen. And, reached by a short passage
running down from the kitchen to the back door, and
situated immediately under the grand flight of stone steps
leading up to the front door, the coal cellar, completely,
sinisterly, dark, containing a miserly scattering of coal
and small quantity of wood, which looked as if it had
been cut from the garden trees. It struck Dew as creepy.

The next day, Saturday 9 July, one of the first things
that he did was to circulate a description of Cora Crippen
as a missing person to every police station in London.

Early on Monday morning, 11 July, Dew and Mitchell
went to Albion House to see Crippen again. He was not
there. Neither was Le Neve. The birds had flown!

It was Dr Gilbert Rylance, an American dentist with
New Zealand qualifications with whom Crippen had
been in business partnership, as the Yale Tooth Specialist
Company, since 1908, who broke the news to Dew. He
had just received the following letter:

Dear Dr Rylance,

I now find that in order to escape trouble I shall be obliged to absent myself for a time.

I believe that with the business as it is now going you will run on all right so far as money matters go ... I shall write you later on more fully.

With kind wishes for your success,

Yours sincerely,

H. H. Crippen.

The flight of Crippen and Le Neve created a huge sensation. During the coming days the newspapers splashed it everywhere. On boats and trains, in trams and buses, in cafés and restaurants, in pubs and clubs it was *the* topic of conversation – speculation, theorising, imaginative constructs. The South London Battersea Murder Mystery paled beside the compulsive fascination of the romantic runaway lovers, the vanished Crippen and Le Neve.

For some obscure prejudicial reason *The Times* would consistently insist on parenthesising the 'Dr' before Crippen's name. The paper was at fault here, for although his medical function and status in this country was lowly, and unseemly his dealings in slightly dubious patent medicines, Crippen was a properly qualified physician. He had enrolled in the School of Homeopathic Medicine at the University of Michigan in 1882, then spent a year in London attending at various hospitals before returning to the States and entering the Homeopathic Hospital in Cleveland, whence he graduated MD in 1884. Then, after studying at the Ophthalmic Hospital in New York, he further qualified, in 1885 taking a degree in eye and ear work. Thereafter, he practised in San Diego and Salt Lake City as an eye and ear specialist. While he was at San Diego he married Charlotte Bell, an Irish-born girl of English parentage, whom he had met as a student nurse at the New York Ophthalmic Hospital.

She bore him a son, Otto Hawley Crippen. She died on 24 January 1892, of apoplexy and paralysis. After her death, Crippen returned to New York and took a position as assistant to a Dr Jeffrey of Brooklyn. It was while working as a general practitioner there that, about the year 1893, he met Cora Turner, who was one of Dr Jeffrey's patients. She was seventeen. Crippen was thirty. She was at that time living under the protection of a Mr C. C. Lincoln, a stove manufacturer, of Water Street, New York. Crippen wooed and won her. Some time after their marriage, at a minister's home in Jersey City, she told him that her name was not Turner, but Kunigunde Mackamotzski. They moved to St Louis, where Crippen practised as consulting physician to an optician named Hirsch, in Olive Street.

In April 1900, after spells in New York, Philadelphia and Toronto, Crippen arrived in London, where he worked at first for Munyon's Remedies, and lived in Queen's Road, St John's Wood. He had left Cora back in New York, where he was paying for her to have her voice trained to sing, as she thought, in grand opera. This was total self-delusion, for she was naturally gifted with no more than a small soprano, sporadically sweetish but constantly weak. Having wisely abandoned ambitions towards opera, she joined him in London in August. They lived for a while at 62 Guildford Street, then in South Crescent, off Tottenham Court Road, and at Nos 34 and 37 Store Street, before, in 1905, renting 39 Hilldrop Crescent, in Holloway.

In 1903 Crippen had severed his connection with Munyon's, and had subsequently gone as manager to the Sovereign Remedy Company at 13 Newman Street. They failed and he went as physician to the Drouet Institution, at Regent's Park and 10 Marble Arch. They also failed. He then secured a position with the Aural Clinic Company, 102 New Oxford Street, and after that went back as manager and advertising manager to

Munyon's, at 272 Oxford Circus, removing with them to Albion House. He was also interested in a business called The Aural Remedy, operating from Craven House, Kingsway.

Leaving Albion House that Monday (11 July), Dew and Mitchell went once more to Hilldrop Crescent. Mademoiselle Lecocq had returned to France, so Dew had to obtain the key to No. 39 from the landlord.

Heavy-mooded with frustration, he and Mitchell laboured again, going through all the tedious automatic routine motions of conscientious search. Then, scrabbling through a wardrobe in the first-floor bedroom, a sudden burst of exhilaration, a sudden discovery ... where nothing of interest had been before, a fully loaded revolver, *and* a box of .45 cartridges that fitted the gun.

Optimism renewed, the searchers went to work with reinvigorated determination, refreshed hope. It persisted throughout a further flat stretch of time – every room re-examined, the garden dug up. Nothing.

Dew was afterwards to claim that the coal cellar was 'one place in the house which had a peculiar fascination for me'. He was now beginning to suspect that Cora Crippen had been murdered. 'Perhaps it was instinct. Anyway, that cellar stuck in my mind. Even in bed, what little I got of it during those hectic days, I couldn't keep my mind from wandering back to the cellar.'

Wednesday, 13 July. 'Let us go along to the house and have another go at the cellar,' said Dew to Mitchell.

Crippen's great mistake was to take flight. If he had stood his ground and gone on living quietly at Hilldrop Crescent, the chances are that the mystery of Cora's disappearance would never have been solved and, as time went on, been forgotten. As it was, within forty-eight hours of receiving the news of Crippen's abscondence, Dew was to find the filleted remains of Belle in the coal cellar.

Down on bended knees, attacking with a sharp-pointed poker the bricks of the cellar floor, Dew found one of them showing signs of having been lifted. Eventually it came up. Then another and another. Mitchell fetched a spade from the garden. Seconds after it bit into the bed of clay below the bricks, the nauseatingly unmistakable stench of decaying flesh cloyed the air. Dew sent for brandy. Fortified by long swigs, he and Mitchell ventured back into the foul-smelling cellar, plied the spade and exposed a mass of putrescent jelly-like flesh, which they thought to be all that remained of the once charming and vivacious erstwhile singing bird, Belle. No head, no limbs, no bones, no genitalia.

Gradually, the immense task of establishing that this big shapeless blob of mouldering tissue was the cadaver of the murdered Cora Crippen was set in motion.

Associated with the rotting flesh they found a Hinde's metal hair-curler, of the kind used by Mrs Crippen. Gripped within its metal jaw was a strand of dark hair, partially dyed light, a fair match for Cora's. Found there, too, were various scraps of a woman's undergarments, a rotting man-size handkerchief, and, most tellingly important of all, a portion of a man's pyjama jacket, bearing the label 'Shirt-makers, Jones Brothers (Holloway), Limited, Holloway, N'.

In a box under the bed in the first-floor bedroom at Hilldrop Crescent, Dew's persistence had yielded two suits of pyjamas, and one odd pair of pyjama trousers, with broad blue stripes. The jackets also bore broad blue stripes, and Jones Brothers' labels.

Dr Augustus Pepper, consulting surgeon at St Mary's Hospital, Paddington, and Home Office pathologist, went to the Islington Mortuary, where the excavated flesh and skin from Hilldrop Crescent had been sent. He examined the material minutely and concluded that it had come from a human of stout build in the prime of life, but it was impossible to sex the remains. He also found that a portion of abdominal skin bore an old operation scar.

Quite by chance, Dew, after attending the formal inquest on Cora, was standing outside the coroner's court close to a group of women who were discussing the case. One of the women was Mrs Paul Martinetti, and Dew pricked up his ears when he overheard her say something about Belle's having had an operation. 'I called Mrs Martinetti to one side and asked her if I had heard aright. "Oh, yes," she replied. "Belle had an operation years ago in America. She had quite a big scar on the lower part of her body. I have seen it."'

Dew told Dr Pepper about the scar, and sometime later microscopic examination was made of a portion of the flesh ... when it was discovered that a scar existed, showing that, whatever body it belonged to, that person had undergone a severe abdominal operation. This, testified to also by Dr Bernard Spilsbury, assisted enormously in the prosecution's contention that the remains found in the cellar were those of Mrs Crippen, and proved to be one of the most important pieces of evidence as to identification.

Further powerful evidence was provided by Dr William Wilcox, senior Home Office scientific analyst, who detected in the remains traces of an alkaloid poison, hyoscine. Investigations revealed that on 19 January Crippen had purchased five grains of hyoscine hydrobromide from Messrs Lewis & Burroughs, the chemist's in New Oxford Street.

On 16 July, the day a warrant was issued at Bow Street Police Station for the arrest of Crippen and Le Neve, Weldon Atherstone or Anderson was murdered. The baffling mystery of his death, which in normal circumstances would without doubt have occasioned very considerable and widespread public attention, was virtually obliterated by the overwhelming interest being displayed in the vanished Crippen and Le Neve, concerning whom an immense hue and cry went up.

Four days later – 20 July – the SS *Montrose* sailed

from Antwerp for Quebec with the fugitives aboard, calling themselves Robinson and disguised as father and son. Something about the couple somehow alerted the suspicion of the skipper of the *Montrose*, Captain Henry Kendall, and he had his Marconi wireless operator send the following message to the managing director of the shipping company, who would pass it on to Scotland Yard:

Montrose. 130 miles West of Lizard.
Have strong suspicion that Crippen London Cellar Murderer and accomplice are amongst saloon passengers. Moustache shaved off, growing beard. Accomplice dressed as boy, voice, manner and build undoubtedly a girl.

Kendall

Dew, exhausted by the relentless and thus far unsuccessful hunt, received in a telegram from the Liverpool police the 'electrifying news', as he called it, that the missing man and woman had been found, and were now under watching eyes somewhere in the safely prisoning waters of the Atlantic.

A notice was issued from Scotland Yard offering a reward of £250 for information which would lead to the arrest of Dr Crippen or Miss Le Neve. Copies of the notice, it was stated, 'will be distributed throughout this country, and will also be sent to all parts of the Continent, printed in French, and to other parts of the world'. A leading official at Scotland Yard – most likely Dew – made a statement to a newspaper representative as to the position of the police in regard to the arrest of Crippen before the discovery of the human remains at Hilldrop Crescent. He said:

People are asking why we allowed the man to remain at liberty, and why we did not arrest him immediately upon visiting the house. The question seems a very simple one, now that it is known to be a case of murder, but before the public pass any condemnation they should try to place themselves in the position we were in before there was any evidence, or any definite suspicion of foul play. Until that time the only intimation we had in our possession was that Mrs Crippen was missing. Well, now, in the course of a week we receive in London alone about a hundred cases of missing people, about whom we are called upon to make inquiries. In this case upon receiving communications from friends of the missing woman, we interviewed Crippen, who told us that his wife had gone off with a count. He spoke in a very off-hand manner, and in effect told us that he did not care in the least that she had gone off with the count since he had the typist to take her place. We were not in a position to enter the house, because we had no evidence of foul play. We were not in the position of the French or American police, who, having greater power than we have, can make an arrest where there is the least ground for suspicion. There is no doubt that we need greater power than we now possess for dealing with cases of murder. If we had entered Crippen's house without his permission, he could have ordered us out, and brought an action against us. As a matter of fact, after he had been closely interrogated Crippen invited us in the house in order that we might search it. We did so, and Crippen himself accompanied us in the search. We found nothing suspicious, and his statement that his wife had gone off with a count suggested a possibility to contradict which we had not then the evidence. As a matter of fact, it was not until Crippen had disappeared that we had any real grounds for suspecting foul play. It was then that we began a thorough search of the house. We were first led to search under the cellar floor by discovering that one or two bricks were loose. It was only then that we obtained evidence of foul play. Before that Mrs Crippen, so far as we were concerned, could only be regarded as one of scores of missing people about whom we are daily making inquiries. If we were less restricted by the law and were given power to arrest where we have the slightest suspicion, we should never hear of a case of this description.

On 23 July Dew and Mitchell sailed from Liverpool on the White Star liner *Laurentic* – a faster ship than the *Montrose* – for Quebec, hoping to overtake their quarry.

The Atlantic chase was on, every nautical mile of it scrutinised by a thoroughly overexcited press. At the pilot station known as Father Point, a desolate outpost of lighthouse, wireless station and wooden shacks on the St Lawrence River, Dew and Mitchell waited in one of the shacks. As the *Montrose* approached, Dew donned a borrowed pilot boat officer's uniform and was rowed out to the *Montrose*, clambering aboard and, in Captain Kendall's cabin, arresting Crippen. He was then escorted to cabin five, where he saw and arrested Ethel Le Neve.

After the conclusion of extradition proceedings, the party left for Liverpool on the *Megantic*, arriving there on 8 August. Hawley Harvey Crippen was put up at the Old Bailey on 18 October 1910. Found guilty, he was hanged at Pentonville on 23 November 1910.

Ethel Clara Le Neve was tried at the Old Bailey on 25 October 1910, on the charge of being an accessory after the fact in the murder of Cora Crippen. She was found not guilty and immediately liberated.

She survived Crippen by fifty-seven years, dying, aged eighty-four, on 9 August 1967, in Dulwich Hospital of heart failure. She had married, on 2 January 1915, Stanley William Smith, a builder's general clerk. They had two children, a son named Robert and a daughter named Nina. Neither of them had the faintest notion of their mother's identity.

Part Six
Inquisitorial

9
The Inquest

The Opening – Tuesday 19 July 1910
The groups clustered about outside the coroner's courts by the Battersea Baths, where Mr John Troutbeck, the coroner for south-west London, was scheduled to open the inquest on Thomas Weldon Anderson at three o'clock that Tuesday afternoon, were largely made up of 'dingy elderly women to whom,' according to the press, 'a tragedy rich in the mysterious seemed to open up a field of wonderment'.

The knots of men were 'mostly of the unemployed sort. They leaned wearily against the palings that divide the railway from the road and seemed not to be particularly interested even in a murder. Two or three motor-cars imported the element of opulence which was necessary to make the scene impressive.'

Shortly after two o'clock – nearly an hour before the inquest was due to begin – droves of reporters were thronging the firmly shut door of the court. When at long last it was opened, the coroner's officer, Police Sergeant Gilbert, took stern control, banishing reporters, who were all set to invade the jury box and were already swarming about the table reserved for the doctors and other professional men involved, to the space at the back of the court normally allocated to witnesses and members of the public.

Long before Mr Troutbeck assumed his seat there was scarcely standing room for the invading legions of late arrival detectives, constables and medical men. Such was the crush that Sergeant Gilbert, pondering the desirability of an injection of fresh air into the foul, stifling atmosphere, decided that 'we shall have to send round to the baths', which enigmatic remark referred to the opening of the cooling battens – a benefit which was distinctly negated by the consequent deafening uproar emanating from an army of schoolchildren rowdily disporting themselves in the baths.

Mr L. Walker, of 73 Kyrle Road, was elected foreman of the jury. Curiously enough the jury was practically the same as that which sat upon the tragic Arding & Hobbs Clapham Junction Department Store fire of 1909.

The twelve good men and true were then hied off to view the body, which lay in the adjacent mortuary. That unpleasant chore disposed of, the coroner announced that he proposed to take only evidence of identification. There was, he said, a good deal of other evidence to be heard, but the police had not got it quite ready. 'We will adjourn the case to an early date and have a day's sitting to contemplate it.'

Although most of the witnesses were in attendance, only one was called – Anderson's sister, Miss Harriet Anderson. Earlier that afternoon she had been sitting weeping in the office downstairs. Beside her had been a tall, alert young man of strikingly attractive personality: the murdered man's elder son, Thomas Frederick Anderson.

Harriet, tall, well built and some forty-nine years of age, was wearing a dark-grey dress, a black hat and black gloves. She read the oath and answered the coroner's questions in a voice stifled with suppressed sobs. She was clearly labouring under severe emotion. Her face was bathed in tears and nearly all the time she was in the witness box she held a little white handkerchief to her eyes. She gave her address as 62 Tufnell Park Road, Upper Holloway.

The coroner then said that he did not intend to go any further with the evidence that day, and asked the jury if the Saturday would be convenient to them. The majority affirmed that it would. He therefore adjourned the inquest until 11 a.m. on 23 July, and the jury was formally bound over to attend. Sergeant Gilbert then proclaimed, 'All interested in this case please leave the court.' There was a great exodus. The jury had to remain to sit on other inquests. When all such business had been concluded, the coroner said that he would not detain them. They could sign all the documents now being prepared on Saturday. One of the jurymen asked if the case would be completed by then. The coroner replied that there would be a great deal of evidence and it would be an all-day sitting.

Said the juryman: 'The majority of us here would not mind sitting late provided they could get the case finished, if possible.'

Another juryman interjected: 'Most of us are going on our holidays.'

'So am I,' said Mr Troutbeck. Then added, 'The place where the death took place is quite close to here. It is very important that you should quite understand the locality. I think if you go and see it you will really find it of very great assistance to you. My officer will take you.'

The jury agreed to go at once.

Second Inquest Sitting – Saturday 23 July 1910

Extraordinary public interest was manifest in the second sitting of the adjourned inquest, and, although proceedings were not due to commence until eleven o'clock, people had begun to collect in the street by nine o'clock. The court was soon opened by its guardians, Sergeant Gilbert and Mr Street, the mortuary superintendent, emerging from their ground-floor office to admit all.

Detective-Inspector Edward Badcock, followed by a sergeant from the Criminal Investigation Department, arrived shortly before the principal witnesses. His mood was adjudged rather more buoyant than at any time since the work of unravelling the mystery had landed in his lap. But beneath that surface air of cheery confidence one suspects an infrastructure of very real anxiety.

It was close on eleven o'clock when Miss Earle and her two companions, a trio in deepest mourning black, drove up in a cab – a closed brougham four-wheeler. There had been some doubt as to whether Miss Earle would be well enough to go through the courtroom ordeal. She had been reported prostrate, and the fact of her absence from Atherstone's funeral had been interpreted as significantly symptomatic of her extreme weakness.

Led by one of her attendant companions, Miss Earle tapped nervously at the locked court door, asking for it to be opened. A little lady, she was extremely pale, much agitated and anxious not to be seen, going head-down, her features hidden behind a fashionable wide-brimmed, heavily veiled hat, yet made conspicuous by her abundance of light auburn hair and string of pearls, standing out luminous against the black of her dress. She turned impatiently away, and, pushing through the crowd, followed by her companions, made her way to the large doors at the Latchmere Road end of the building. Meanwhile, Sergeant Gilbert quickly opened the door and called to the ladies to return. Miss Earle seemed to be on the verge of collapse as one of her friends seized her arm and practically lifted her into the court precincts, where she entered a waiting room. As soon as the ladies had been shown into the waiting room the reporters were admitted. Atherstone's two sons, Thomas Frederick and William Gordon, soon arrived in a friend's motor car.

The court was again crowded. The first business of the resumed inquest dealt with locality – the proving of plans of the premises where the crime had taken place – and the first witness called to that end was Police Constable George Franklin, 921 V Division of the Metropolitan Police, who acted as presenter. He it was who put in plans of the ground-floor flat at No. 17 Prince of Wales Road, the scene of the crime, and its immediate vicinity.

There were four plans, drawn to scale, which included the floor area of the ground-floor flat; a long passage by the side of the house; the walls, which were four feet six inches high; and the scullery door, which was six feet six inches high and two feet six inches wide.

Divisional Detective Inspector Edward Badcock, who was in overall charge of the case, gave evidence of the photographing of the premises by an officer from Scotland Yard. The seven photographs showed the rear of the flats at No. 17 Prince of Wales Road and the garden of Cambridge House (No. 19 Prince of Wales Road), which is the last house in the Clifton Gardens block and stands at the corner of Prince of Wales Road and Rosenau Road.

One of the photographs showed footprints of someone apparently coming from Rosenau Road to the back of No. 17.

The jury were especially fascinated by the photographs of the murderer's footprints, which were explained to them by Inspector Badcock. The traces were actually so indistinct that Badcock had to walk across to the jury box and actually point out what were taken to be footprints.

Next came three witnesses graphically describing the flight of the fugitive. The triumvirate was disappointingly variant, yielding minimal useful consensus. Noice was pre-eminently aware of the indistinct figure of a man. Mrs Lewis carried away the overriding image of a soft, round, white moon face. Mr Jones registered a young man, not of the labouring class, slim, slight, about five feet tall. No stamp of remarkability. No illuminative singularity. All agreed that he wore a lounge suit; dark tweed said Edward Noice, soiled said Mrs Emma Lewis, dark echoed Arthur Jones.

Noice testified that at about 9.30 p.m. on Saturday 16 July, he had heard two shots fired in quick succession. He was walking along Rosenau Road at the time, on the pavement of the side opposite to Cambridge House. His home, No. 45 Rosenau Road, where he had been living for the last six months or so, was some fifty yards from Cambridge House. It was very dark and, although there was an electric standard about fifty or sixty yards away from the garden wall of Cambridge House, he could not see distinctly. He could just make out a man breaking through the trees in Cambridge House garden. He next saw him on top of the Cambridge House garden wall in Rosenau Road, drop on to the pavement, turn to the left, pelt up to Petworth Street, and run very fast towards the Albert Bridge and the river.

Noice had been unable to form any impression of him, other than that he was about five feet six inches tall, and he could see that he was not a labourer. He could not say whether he was fat or thin, or whether he was or was not wearing a hat. He might have worn a cap. He definitely wore no overcoat. He carried nothing in his hands. He must, in fact, have used both hands to get over the wall, which was, Noice said, about seven feet high. 'He had to drop over, and that enabled me to judge his height. When his hands were on the top his feet were not touching the ground.' Noice said that he saw the body of the deceased that evening and it was not that of a man whom he had ever seen before. Neither had he ever before seen the man who got over the wall.

Mrs Lewis, a housekeeper, of 24 Juer Street, Battersea, was the next witness. She said that at about 9.30 p.m. that Saturday while walking along Rosenau Road, she heard two loud reports. There was about a second between the shots. She looked over the wall in Rosenau Road to see if she could see anything, and to her surprise saw a man spring over the wall. He landed only a step away from her, and ran off at speed in the direction of the river. She estimated the man to have been five feet three inches tall. He had no overcoat, but was wearing a dark jacket suit, and, she thought, a bowler hat. He carried nothing in his hands, and wore no gloves. She could not say if he had any hair on his face. She did not hear him say anything. She thought that she could recognise him again, but only by his back or the side of his face. After his disappearance she had gone across the road and spoken with Noice.

The third witness was Arthur Jones, a salesman of 44A Isis Street, Earlsfield. He said that at about 9.30 p.m. on Saturday 16 July he had been going home from work, walking along Rosenau Road towards Battersea Park Road. When opposite No. 40 or 42, he heard two revolver shots fired in quick succession.

As he got opposite to No. 12, a man of about his own build came by him, running and breathing very hard. He ran towards Petworth Street. Jones thought at the time that someone had committed suicide and that the man was running for a doctor. He had just caught a passing glimpse of the man's face. He could not say if he had any hair on it, but if he had it was a fair moustache. He was wearing a cap and a jacket. Jones did not think that the man had anything in his hands. Nor did he notice anything about his boots, but he thought 'they were light, because they made very little noise as he was running. I didn't hear him until he was practically on top of me.' Jones considered it unlikely that the man would be a labourer – 'His clothes were similar to what I have got on [dark]. I should sooner say he was a clerk than a labourer.' He judged him to be between twenty and thirty years of age, slim and light, and added, 'There was nothing to call any special attention to him.'

Police Sergeant William Buckley, 105 V, who was the first police officer on the scene and put the time of his call at the police station as 9.35 p.m. said that he had proceeded in a motor car, accompanied by Noice and a man named Harold Glanville, of 41 Rosenau Road, to the flats at No. 17 Prince of Wales Road. He had there endeavoured to enter the ground-floor flat, but was unable to do so. He next went up to the first floor and knocked at the door. It was opened by Miss Elizabeth Earle.

I said to her, 'I have received information that two shots have been fired at the rear of these premises. Will you allow me to come through your flat and make a search?'

She replied, 'Yes. I heard the shots and saw a man climb over the wall.'

Sergeant Buckley continued:

I entered the flat and in passing through the kitchen to get to the back stairs I saw a man whom I now know as Thomas Frederick Anderson. He said, 'I'll go with you.'

I went down the iron staircase leading to the backyard, followed by Anderson, and in company with him I searched in the vicinity where the man got over the wall, also several other yards. Coming back to the yard of No. 17, I came to the wall that separates the two houses, Cambridge House and No. 17 Prince of Wales Road. I was looking over the wall to see if I could find any traces of anyone when Anderson walked up the steps as if to go into the kitchen again. He called to me and said, 'There is a man lying here.'

I walked towards Anderson and saw there was a man lying on the scullery steps of the ground-floor flat with his legs out in the yard. I got a light first. I asked Anderson to get a light. Miss Earle, who was standing at the top of the staircase, said, 'I'll get you a lamp.' The lamp was then lighted by Anderson. I then saw the man had a small shot wound on the side of his face. Anderson held the light for me. I might add that the man was lying on his back with his head turned to the left.

There was nothing on his head. Not much blood about his face. The bleeding on the left side had practically ceased when I got there. He was unconscious, but still breathing. I turned his head to the right, and then I saw he had a shot wound on the left temple and his eye was hanging on his left cheek. I noticed that the first shot went in the mouth and came out of the right cheek.

I asked Anderson to send for a doctor. Noice went and brought back Dr Marrett, of Clifton House, 58 Cambridge Road, Battersea Park. I also sent for Dr Kempster, the divisional police surgeon, and sent information to the police station.

The man died at 10.20 p.m. without regaining consciousness. Dr Kempster was present at the death.

Buckley said that the dead man was fully dressed in a blue serge suit and had on his feet a pair of plaited felt carpet slippers with soft soles.

Answering the coroner, Buckley said that up to that time deceased had not been identified by anyone. 'I have left one thing out,' he said. 'I asked Anderson when we first got the light if he knew of anyone answering the description of the man, and he replied, 'No.'

'So far as you could judge was there great disfigurement of the face?' asked Mr Troutbeck.

'No, not on the right side. There had just been a little trickling of blood from the wound. All the disfigurement was on the left side.'

'Where,' asked the coroner, 'was Miss Earle all this time?'

'She came halfway down the stairs with the lamp and went back again.'

'Did she see the body then?'

'No. I told her there was a man shot and if she was nervous not to come down.'

Coroner: 'Did you notice the window of the backyard?'
Buckley: 'No.'

Coroner: 'Was the scullery door shut?'

Buckley: 'It was half-open – at an angle of about forty-five degrees.'

Coroner: 'Was the front door of the flats open when you entered?'

Buckley: 'The outside, front street door is open day and night. It is an entrance used by the occupiers of the three flats.'

The foreman of the jury asked, 'Did Miss Earle or the son seem agitated when you told them why you had come?'

Buckley: 'No.'

Foreman: 'They made no further remarks about seeing the man go over the wall?'

Buckley: 'No.'

Detective Inspector Emmanuel Geake was the next witness to be called. He had, he said, been on night duty at Battersea Police Station when he was informed at 9.45 p.m. by Harold Glanville that a man had been shot at the back of No. 17 Prince of Wales Road, and that a man had been seen running away. He immediately sent for the divisional police surgeon, Dr Kempster, and, taking four constables and a police ambulance with him, set off at once for the scene. He entered the slender strip of front garden, and jumped over a four-foot wall into a passageway that ran between Nos 17 and 19 Prince of Wales Road. He proceeded up the passage and, jumping over the higher reaches of the same four-foot wall, succeeded in getting into the rear of No. 17, where he saw Dr Marrett and Sergeant Buckley attending to the injured man. 'I was told that the body had been pulled up a little, so that the head rested on the scullery step. Otherwise the body was lying on its back.'

He posted constables around the house and sent telegrams to the divisional superintendent and Divisional Detective Inspector Badcock. He also made inquiries as to whether the injured man was known locally.

Receiving negative replies, he kept the witnesses in the house and made sure that no one was permitted to enter the gardens.

The injured man having died at 10.20 p.m., it now became a case of murder, and Geake told young Anderson that he would have to take a statement from him.

Time was getting on and Anderson was worried. 'I have to be in by 11.30 or I shall be locked out. Can I leave my name and address?'

Geake said, 'No.'

At about half-past eleven Anderson came outside saying, 'I feel sick stopping inside. I want some fresh air.'

Geake called him over and asked: 'Do you know a man named Atherton?'

'No,' he replied, 'I know Atherstone.'

Geake had then referred to a card which Detective Sergeant Purkiss had found on the deceased, and on being shown it Anderson said, 'That's my father's card.' Whereupon Geake had told him that he would take him to the station, pending inquiries.

The coroner interjected: 'Up to that time he did not know who it was? When he recognised the card was he allowed to see the body?'

Geake said that he had thought that it was young Anderson's father, but he had not thought at the time to take him back to see the body.

Inspector Badcock interrupted, saying, 'He saw it at the mortuary the following day [Sunday 17th].'

Turning to Geake, the coroner observed, 'You assumed, I suppose, that the moment that the card was recognised the identification was made out?

Geake agreed.

'Did Anderson say anything else?'

'He said, "Is that my father that was shot?" I said, "I don't know. You were there." He asked, "Has he got a false moustache on?" I said, "No, he is clean-shaven." He said, "I can't think it is my father." I said, "I don't know. I want you to realise that you are detained in order that inquiries may be made; for nothing else at present." He then burst into a fit of crying, and putting his hands up to his face, exclaimed, "Good God, it is my father!"'

The coroner: 'He had seen the body and had not recognised it. There was nothing further except the production of that card to make him say that and brought about the identification?'

Geake: 'Yes, it was merely this card.'

The inspector went on to tell the court that there were certain significant points arising out of one of the entries in a memorandum book, which had been found in the deceased's pocket, and in which he seemed to have kept a diary.

One entry which we have already considered and which much exercised Geake, was:

> If he had kept away from her, if he had broken from the spell of her fascination and remained out of reach, this would never have happened. He has no one to thank but himself. We all reap as we have sown.

This in fact turned out to be a quotation copied from *The Smart Set*, a well-known monthly literary magazine founded in America in March 1900, whither its origin was traced by Atherstone's elder son, Thomas Frederick Anderson. There followed, too, several short dissertations on love, which were also obviously copied from printed sources.

This aforementioned excerpt was one of them:

> The prime essence of love is that it should be complete, making no reservation and allowing no check from the reason. When the heart gets the mastery it knows neither rest nor mercy. If the heart is good the result will be good; if bad, evil.

The coroner asked if Miss Earle had seen this 'diary'. Geake said that she had, and that she had been questioned about it.

'What you suggest,' said the coroner, 'is that the entries indicate jealousy of Miss Earle.'

'Yes,' answered Geake. Then, abruptly changing the topic, he went on to say that he had compared the boots of the deceased with the footprints in the gardens, and that they quite definitely did not correspond.

Commented Mr Troutbeck: 'However the deceased got in, there is nothing to suggest he came through the garden.'

The foreman of the jury asked: 'Have you any idea how he got in?'

Geake told him, 'I found the piece of cord protruding from the letterbox on the bottom flat. That was attached to the latch of the door, and would have enabled anyone to open the door from the outside. It was attached by the workmen who had been repairing the flat.'

Geake was followed in the witness box by Detective Sergeant Harry Purkiss of V Division, who deposed to his having gone to the rear of No. 17 at about 10.30 p.m. on the Saturday (16th) and conducted a careful search of the body and clothing of the deceased actor. In the hip pocket he found a latchkey and a piece of insulated electric cable, about seventeen inches long. It was wrapped tightly in brown paper, and bound round and round with string, with a loop at the end for the wrist. A formidable cosh-like weapon or 'life preserver', it was running up the back between Atherstone's waistcoat and coat.

In the inside right-hand breast pocket there were several letters addressed to 'Weldon Atherstone, Esq., 14 Great Percy Street, W.C.' A red memorandum book contained a visiting card, 'T. Weldon Atherstone, Leading Character Actor, 14 Great Percy Street, W.C.' In the same pocket was a handkerchief and an empty spectacle case.

In the left waistcoat pocket was an English gold watch with a strap chain. In the right waistcoat pocket were two keys and a small piece of comb. In the left jacket pocket was a pipe, tobacco pouch, a box of matches and a packet of cigarette papers. In the right trouser pocket was 2s 11d in money – half a crown in silver and five pence in bronze.

Purkiss said that he afterwards saw young Anderson at the Battersea Police Station. Anderson asked him, 'Will you describe the dead man to me?' Purkiss said, 'He is a man about my height; round, thin face, similar to your own; and clean-shaven.' Anderson began to cry and said, 'Good God, I saw my father die.'

Detective Sergeant John Parker, of V Division, stepped into the box to carry the matter further with his account of Atherstone's two sons' visit to the Battersea Mortuary at Sheepcote Lane, at 8.30 a.m. on Sunday 17 July. He told of their seeing and identifying the body of their father, and how he had pointed to the felt slippers, still on the corpse's feet, and William Anderson had said, 'To the best of my belief, they are the slippers I saw my father wearing at his lodgings on 2 July.'

As officer in charge of the case, Detective Inspector Edward Badcock was an important figure. He had been called in to head the investigation shortly after eleven o'clock on the night of the murder. He was sitting with Detective Sergeant Pusey at a table that was loaded with evidential material. There were bundles of letters and piles of documents. One packet was labelled 'Tram Tickets', another contained scraps of paper or other apparently worthless trifles picked up at the flat, and the bullets from the assassin's revolver were close at hand. But all this accumulation was practically valueless.

Badcock explained,

I examined the premises and found a hole in the window of the ground-floor scullery door, and an indentation on the partition between the two panes of glass next to the hole. In a sink behind the open scullery door, I found two pieces of the bullet [produced]. About eight feet from the back door, I picked up three pieces of a spectacle frame. There were a number of crushed pieces of glass near, but none that I could recognise as belonging to the spectacles. The hole through the glass panel was 4 ft. 3 1/2 in from the floor of the scullery. Two steps leading to the scullery door were a foot high together.

After further examination of the premises, Badcock had gone up to Miss Earle's flat and interrogated her. 'I took her statement down in writing.'

A juryman asked how Atherstone had got into the ground-floor flat. Badcock explained how the decorators had fixed up a piece of cord which, attached to the latch inside, protruded through the letterbox and when pulled lifted the latch, thus releasing the door.

He now produced a small red diary, which he said had been found in Atherstone's pocket, the entries in which clearly indicated the deceased's jealousy of Miss Earle. He said that Miss Earle had been shown the memorandum book and questioned on it. 'She does not say that she knows the book.'

Coroner: 'What you suggest is that these entries intimate jealousy of Miss Earle?'

Badcock agreed.

The coroner, having examined the diary, turned to the jury and, telling them, 'These are intimate entries, Gentlemen,' passed copies of some of the entries to the jury, who made a long inspection of them.

It was when replying to an interruption by the coroner as he was reading out Miss Earle's statement to the Court, that Badcock said that Miss Earle had handed to him a postcard in confirmation of what she had said about the appointment with young Anderson.

He went on to detail how, as daylight broke, he had

examined the garden of Cambridge House and found there impressions of a man's boots, size nine. They were immediately under the wall by Rosenau Road, and were pointing in the direction of No. 17. There were two similar, but lighter, impressions pointing in the direction of Rosenau Road. On the opposite side of the garden there were also a number of indistinct footmarks, leaves broken off the bough of a tree, and marks on the Virginia creeper on the trellis work. 'It appeared to me to indicate that someone had come from the opposite side. There was a mark on the ledge of the greenhouse and the wall, as if someone had passed from the garden of Cambridge House into the yard at the rear of 17 Prince of Wales Road.'

Following a short adjournment, during which press and public filed out to wait in the street, it was the turn of the doctors; time for the medical evidence.

Dr Felix Charles Kempster, the divisional police surgeon, a general practitioner, of 59 Battersea Bridge Road, deposed that at 9.45 p.m. he had been called to No. 17 Prince of Wales Road. At the rear of the ground-floor flat he saw the body of a man whom he now knew as Weldon Anderson. The body was lying at right angles to the scullery steps. There were two wounds, one in the upper lip, and one in the left temple. Both had been bleeding at 9.35 p.m. He had bandaged the injured man's head and stayed with him until he died. He lived until 10.20 p.m., although he remained unconscious. At that time the man's face was not much disfigured. 'Young Anderson came up as I was examining the body. He was there for some considerable time. The features were quite placid, and when the body was seen next morning, and recognised by the son, the body was in exactly the same state.'

Coroner: 'Was there a good light?'

Kempster: 'A splendid light.'

Kempster said that in his opinion the cause of death

was coma, following upon concussion and laceration of the brain due to a bullet wound. The bullet had been fired at quite close quarters at the head of the deceased. Powder marks, well defined, were visible over the wound, and, less well marked, they were also visible round the wound near the mouth. The shot had entered at the outer angle of the left eyebrow, and, passing backwards and to the right, was found loose in the skull. The bullet that entered near the mouth was found in the scullery sink. There were fingernail marks on the face and on the wrists. Judging by the complete absence of any blood on the fingernails of the deceased, the scratches were made by his assailant. There was every indication of a struggle having taken place previous to the shots being fired. The weapon used was apparently a revolver or small pistol.

When the body was turned over he had observed a tweed cap beneath it. The cap had been identified by one of the sons. He had observed that the man was wearing plaited felt slippers. He had noticed a bullet mark on the wooden beading of the glass panelling of the downstairs scullery door. There was a circular smash in the glass, which had flaked off inwards, showing that the bullet had come from the outside. He had also registered the fact that neither the latch nor the bolt of the scullery door had been forced.

Dr Ludwig B. Freyberger, of 9 St Mark's Square, Regent's Park, toxicologist and pathologist to the London County Council, had carried out the post-mortem on Atherstone at 4 p.m. on Sunday 17 July, assisted by Dr Kempster. He corroborated Dr Kempster's given cause of death. He told the court that although the deceased, a fairly muscular man, was said to be forty-seven, he was grey-haired and looked much older than his years.

There had been a severe recent bruise on the lower end of deceased's back, evidently caused by a heavy fall. It extended through the skin to the muscle. He thought that the lip wound was merely a flesh wound, passing through the region of the upper lip. It was not a disabling wound. He had found marks on the chest. In his opinion they were due to friction, the rubbing of the man's shirt, probably in the course of a struggle. The police had detected bruises round the dead man's mouth that in their view exactly corresponded to the thumb and four fingers of a 'spread' hand, such as would have been left if the murderer had tried to close his opponent's mouth and prevent an outcry.

The coroner sent his officer to interview Elizabeth Earle with regard to the accident sustained by Atherstone to which she had referred in her statement. On his return Gilbert said that he had been informed by Miss Earle that Atherstone had been knocked down two years before by a motor car. He had been very much bruised, and suffered from slight concussion. He had been taken to hospital, where he had remained for about three hours.

Atherstone's sixteen-year-old son, William Gordon, was called. He was a pale, fragile-looking youth apprenticed as a warehouseman to Messrs Foster Porter & Co., Ltd, Wholesale Drapery Warehousemen, and since October 1909 had been living at their premises at 47 Wood Street, E.C. He said that his father had no particular residence in town, as he was an actor travelling the country. He could not say where he generally stayed when he was in London. It would be in different places. With Miss Earle sometimes.

William said that he had last seen his father around midday on the fatal Saturday at his Great Percy Street lodgings, where he had been staying with his father during his fortnight's holiday – the last two weeks of his father's life. That afternoon he had gone to Willesden, where he attended a cricket match with friends. He had been told of the tragedy at 2 a.m. on Sunday 17 July by two detectives, who had then taken him to Battersea Police Station. He had not seen his brother there until later on. His brother had told him that the reason why he had not recognised his father at first was because of a blood mark on the upper lip which he had thought was a moustache, and, in any event, his father was the last person he had expected to see there. He said that his father was a man of sober habits, that he had never had a revolver in his possession and that he had no reason to think he was on bad terms with anyone.

On Wednesday (13th) night he was away all night. He had said that he had 'private business', and when he arrived home next morning said that he had had 'no luck'. He came home by workman's tram (the ticket was produced). The ticket had been issued in the Battersea district. Young William said that he, his brother and his father had a conversation on Thursday (14th) in a house in Finsbury Park. Mr Troutbeck asked Anderson if he had given the police the name of the place in Finsbury Park where Thomas Frederick had told his father that he was to be going to see Miss Earle on the Saturday evening.

Anderson: 'I believe so.'

However, Detective Sergeant Pusey informed the court that the police had not got that address, and, at the coroner's request, Anderson wrote it down.

'Is this a friend of yours?' asked the coroner.

'No; a friend of the family.'

There is no mystery about the Finsbury Park premises. Interviewed, the lady of the house said:

We have known Mr Anderson and the members of his family for quite a number of years. We all respected Mr Anderson highly. He was one of the finest men you could meet, and, in particular, we all admired him for the interest and affection which he bestowed upon his children. The meeting which took place at my house on the evening of the 14th inst. was arranged in the last resort by telephone. It was simply an informal visit. Mr Anderson with his younger son, called about a quarter to eight, and the elder came along a little later. We had a chat and some supper, and I think we spent some little time in the garden. I saw nothing in the least unusual in Mr Anderson's manner that night. There was no sign whatever of any trouble hanging over him – none of the moodiness of brooding jealousy or vengeance. He was just his own affable self. It was altogether a happy gathering. I think the allusion to the elder son's contemplated call upon Miss Earle arose in this way. I suggested that they should all call upon us again on the Saturday (16th) in order that we might have a group photograph taken in our garden. Then it was that the elder son mentioned that he was very sorry he could not come as he had arranged to pay a visit to Miss Earle. And that is the whole story.

So ... the elements of mystery and weighty portent that were read into the family gathering in Finsbury Park come to nothing at all when they are inquired into. They are defused.

Continuing his evidence regarding the last fortnight of his father's life, William went on: 'I generally went with him to the theatrical offices in the Strand.' Young Anderson added that during the fortnight's holiday that he spent with his father, he (the father) never spoke to Miss Earle, nor did he speak of her. Nor did he go to Battersea, so far as William knew.

Answering the coroner, William Anderson said that he knew Miss Earle fairly well. He saw her when he was very young, and saw her about three or four months ago. His brother was, he said, a greater friend of hers than he was. He knew of no reason why he had not seen her since; he had not had time.

Coroner: 'You could have gone to see her during the last fortnight.'

Anderson: 'Yes, but I didn't think of it.'

Coroner: 'She speaks of her relationship as if she were a mother to you two boys.'

Anderson: 'Yes, she was. She took a great interest in us.'

He had heard of no estrangement between Miss Earle and his father.

Mr Troutbeck said that there was still a considerable amount of evidence to be taken, including that of Miss Earle, whose examination would take some time. The police authorities also desired further time for the prosecution of certain lines of evidence they proposed to follow up. Their suggestion was that there should be an adjournment for at least three weeks. 'Some of you said something about holidays last time. I don't want to bring any of you back from your holidays.'

After consultation with his colleagues, the coroner said, 'The twenty-first of August seems to be the latest day.'

He then, at 4.45 p.m., adjourned the inquest until 17 September. Before his binding over the jury to be in their places on the date, it was announced that William Gordon Anderson desired to make a further statement. He went into the witness box, and explained that his father's expression 'bad luck' meant his business.

In the interval between the end of the second sitting and the onset of the final inquest sitting the rumour-mongers got to work. It was reported that Elizabeth Earle was about to undergo an operation, and that upon her recovery she intended to be off to Australia to join her brother. She was found to be absent from her flat, and it was bruited abroad that she had already set slyly forth on her antipodean odyssey. Nothing of the sort; with the permission of the police she had gone to recuperate with friends in Normandy.

Third and Final Inquest Sitting – Saturday 17 September 1910

The coroner arrived early, hurrying into court to avoid questions which were being levelled at him.

Miss Earle drove up in a cab. She was dressed in deep black again, and heavily veiled. She and the friend who accompanied her remained in the cab until the doors of the building were opened. A seemingly well-meaning and obliging photographer assisted Miss Earle out of the hansom, doubtless with the idea of making things easy for his colleagues, who were set on getting pictures of her; but Miss Earle, pulling her hat down over her face, thus easily aborted the well-meaning one's scheme and scurried into the court, unphotographed.

Next to arrive was Thomas Frederick Anderson, quickly followed by his brother, William Gordon. Then came Mr C. O. Humphreys, solicitor, announcing that he represented Miss Earle.

The Borough News reported, 'Pressmen were there in great body, Press Artists stealthily sketching. Doctors and a sprinkling of men of the law, while behind all those who had some kind of official interest in the case, were ranked a group of eager faces belonging to that small proportion of the general public who had succeeded in obtaining admittance.'

The first witness to give evidence was Thomas Frederick Anderson (recalled). He was tall, thin-faced and somewhat delicate-looking, with a receding chin and a very large and prominent nose. Twenty-one years old, he was dressed in a well-fitting blue reefer suit, clearly of highly strung nervous temperament and still obviously suffering from the shock of his terrible ordeal; nevertheless, he contrived to give his evidence with outward composure.

He said that he lived at 119 [*sic*] Wood Street, E.C., where he was a warehouseman's assistant. He told the court that up to two years ago [i.e. 1908] Miss Earle's brother had also lived in her flat. His father, he said, lived in London for four or more months of the year – when not on tour. About two years ago he had stayed in Edgware Road and at an address in Stratford E. Also at

King's Cross for the convenience of his engagements. The reason why his father had ceased to stay with Miss Earle at Christmas 1909 was because of a difference of opinion about his meeting one of her friends – a male friend and his wife. The difference had been surmounted.

His father had again ceased to stay with Miss Earle at Whitsuntide 1910, because he had to be in the Strand a good deal on business and thought it would be more convenient, Battersea being a long way away. His father had come to London for the last time in May 1910. Whit Sunday was on 15 May. He had stayed with Miss Earle for a few days, and then went to 14 Great Percy Street. From Whitsuntide until a few weeks before his death he had been giving turns at various music halls in London.

Mr Humphreys asked Thomas, 'Do you know if your father was on similar terms of intimacy with any other person?' and 'Had your father any personal enemy?'

Thomas replied in the negative to both questions. He agreed that if he had known of the relations between his father and Miss Earle he would probably not have visited her. He was not aware of the terms upon which his mother and father had separated. He had last seen his mother at Easter 1909.

When Anderson had completed his evidence, the coroner said, 'Call Miss Earle.' An audible stir went through the court. She was the witness everyone was anxious to see and hear. She walked in with dignity from the waiting room. Though she held her head erect, she kept her thick veil drawn while walking into the court, and upon taking a seat in the witness box arranged herself in such a position that only the coroner could see her face.

Said the *News of the World* of 18 September:

Nothing could have been more mournful than the entry into the court of Miss Earle. A diminutive, thin, shrinking figure, she was dressed completely in deep mourning, with her face shrouded in a thick black veil. She moved slowly under a weight of great grief to the witness-box. Her face was very thin. She delivered her evidence in an expressionless monotone and in a voice of such low pitch that the coroner was repeatedly obliged to request her to speak more loudly. The coroner had also to ask her to raise her veil that she might be heard more clearly, and it was then that one saw her tiny features, drawn with the nerve strain of the proceedings. The story of her relationship with the deceased, his mad jealousy and outbreaks of violence, she told fully and with considerable feeling, frequently being on the verge of breaking into tears.

Another reporter wrote,

She was not the woman many expected to see, but a person of great susceptibility and delicate refinement, without suspicion of loudness in taste or manner. A woman of deep feeling, she had suffered much, and the suffering had irradically marked her pale face, but her fortitude and calmness were admirable. ... All that she knew she stated without equivocation, and though some of the questions on which she was publicly questioned must have caused her pain she did not flinch. Only when dealing with her relations with Mr Anderson did her features relax, and then, too, her eyes were more than once swelled with tears. Whatever the feelings of the actor might have been with regard to her, it is certain that she had for him a devoted self-sacrificing affection. Once she intimated, with a sincerity none could doubt, that her one object had been to make him happy.

She said that she had had private pupils of both sexes at her flat. She had given the police the names of the pupils. She gave up the male pupils twelve months last June (i.e. 1909), because she did not want to do anything to offend Mr Anderson.

Mr Humphreys: Did the fact (that she was taking private pupils) seem to affect Mr Anderson?

Miss Earle: Yes. He felt that our lives were going separately, and that we were having different interests.

Mr Humphreys: And that he was being shut out?

Miss Earle: Yes.

Mr Humphreys: It was not so was it?

Miss Earle: No.

Mr Humphreys: But is it to that that you attribute this unreasoning jealousy on his part?

Miss Earle: That was the beginning of it.

The coroner asked, 'Did you do this [give up the male pupils] because of his threat, or were you frightened?'

'No, I was not frightened, but I did not want to make him unhappy.'

Answering Mr Humphreys, Miss Earle agreed that it had been so as to avoid all questions between herself and Anderson that she ceased to take male pupils. She had had to take private work in order to keep her invalid brother in Australia. She gave her evidence in a tragic voice, which was not always easily heard.

She was, she said, a teacher of expression at the Academy of Dramatic Art, in Gower Street – this was to become RADA, the Royal Academy of Dramatic Art. She had been living at her present address for four years, and previously lived in the flat below. She had known the deceased for eleven years, and ten years ago began to live on intimate terms with him. He used to come and stay with her. They had lived on good terms together, but during the last four years there had been quarrels. The reason, she said, was that he was jealous – 'jealous of every man I knew. I never gave him any reason or cause for jealousy'. There was no one she knew who was paying her any particular attention. Notwithstanding these quarrels, she continued her intimate relations with him up to eight weeks before his death. They ceased because 'Mr Anderson said I had someone staying with me. I denied it, and he struck and left me'.

The separation was by his wish, not Miss Earle's.

'He called that night and brought the key back and left his address for letters to be sent. He left a letter:

Dear Bessie – Just to enclose latchkey and give my address, to which you can forward any letters if they turn up. I am so sorry I hurt you, very sorry. Of course you can but deny that was the ground you were forced to take. I am sorry.

The coroner asked: 'Do you know whether he ever came into your flat?'

'Only from the entries in his diary,' she replied. 'They lead me to think that he had been in since the rupture.'

'How did he get in?'

It was stated that the key had been found on the body, and the coroner said that he might have had this one specially cut. It certainly looked newer, and the shape was longer.

Miss Earle said that as far as she knew he had had only one key, which he had given out. He had, however, often come in at the back (that is to say up the iron staircase and in at the scullery door). It was not necessary for him to have the key, because the scullery back door was always open, never locked.

The coroner said that he understood there had been burglars in the district and asked her if she had been visited.

'Yes, I had my gas meter broken open last year. They broke in at the front door.'

The coroner observed, 'You did not think it necessary to shut your back door after that?'

'No,' said Miss Earle.

Mr Troutbeck asked her if she could give any information to assist in finding out the person who shot

Atherstone. She said that she could not. She had told the police everything. She had no idea at all who had done it. Deceased had been in a peculiar state of mind lately. She did not know if in that peculiar state of mind he had got on bad terms with anybody other than herself.

Coroner: 'I think he had mentioned several men in connection with yourself? You say there is no reason?'

Miss Earle: 'Nothing at all.'

Coroner: 'Did he ever attack or question any of these men?'

Miss Earle: 'Not to my knowledge.'

Coroner: 'Have you any suggestions as to why he had this weapon, this piece of electric cable upon him?'

Miss Earle said that she had no idea.

Coroner: 'He had been violent to you once?'

Miss Earle: 'More than once.' She said that he had struck her in a sudden rage. 'He once threatened to cut my throat. That was last summer [1909].'

Coroner: 'I don't want to go into details as to the entries in this diary, as they are rather of an intimate nature, and show that he was watching you, do they not?'

Miss Earle: 'Yes.'

Coroner: 'I understand there have been burglars in the district?'

Mr Humphreys returned to the subject as he wanted to establish the fact that there had been serious burglaries in the district.

Miss Earle again said that there had, that she had been visited by them last year and had had her gas meter broken open and thirteen shillings stolen from it. The burglars had got in at her front door.

Inspector Badcock, replying to Mr Humphreys, said that there were frequent thefts from gas meters in the neighbourhood, and meters on the top and bottom premises had been broken into. The occupants of flats often opened them.

A juror: 'But they don't commit murder.'

Badcock: 'No, neither do meter thieves commit murders. When we get them they are invariably men who have fallen out of work and are suddenly tempted to go upstairs and rob a neighbour's meter, or else they are youths. A practical thief does not rob a gas meter.'

Miss Earle told the court that when she heard the shots she 'thought they were shooting cats, and … jumped up and looked out of the scullery door'. Then she had said, 'Someone has fired a shot to scare off a burglar.' She thought that the weapon used was 'one of those old-fashioned pistols that make a lot of noise and do not do any damage.'

After young Anderson had been taken to Battersea Police Station, an officer asked Miss Earle if her name was 'Bess', and she replied, 'Yes.' She was then asked if she knew anyone of the name of Atherstone, and she said that she did. 'He is the dead man,' said the officer. That was the first time she knew who the deceased was. It was a terrible shock.

Questioned by Mr Troutbeck as to her opinion of Atherstone's mental state, Miss Earle said: 'I think he had got this idea [of her infidelity] into his head, and it had become an obsession.' She said that two years ago the deceased met with a motor-car accident. It was on 14 January 1908 that he was knocked down in Pimlico. He suffered slight concussion of the brain, but nothing sufficiently serious to require his being more than two or three hours in hospital.

Coroner: 'Was there any noticeable alteration in his manner after the accident?'

Miss Earle: 'Yes. There was a noticeable increase in his fits of jealousy.'

The coroner again asked Miss Earle if she could give any information to assist in finding out the person who shot Atherstone. Again, she said that she could not. She had told the police everything. She had no idea at all who had done it.

Her testimony completed, gratefully Miss Earle stepped down.

Thomas Frederick Anderson took her place in the witness box. The coroner went with him through the events of the fatal Saturday evening. Young Anderson said that when he arrived at Miss Earle's flat at eight o'clock, she let him in at the front entrance. 'We went into the drawing room' – the front room overlooking Prince of Wales Road – 'talking for some time, and then she said she would go and get some supper ready. This would be a quarter to nine. While out in the kitchen she called to me and showed me the new fittings in her bedroom. We came back from there to the drawing-room and talked a little longer.'

The coroner asked: 'What were the new fittings?'

Anderson: 'The room had been new papered and there were new curtains.'

Coroner: 'Had you been in her bedroom before?'

Anderson: 'Yes. We returned to the drawing room and following that we went to the kitchen for supper. That would be about nine o'clock. Miss Earle was preparing supper and we sat down. That would be about a quarter past nine. We had been seated at supper a short time when we heard two loud reports.'

Coroner: 'Just tell me where the kitchen is. Where does the window look on to?'

Anderson: 'It looks on to the staircase which runs to the scullery door.'

Coroner: 'The kitchen window looks sideways on to the passage?'

Anderson: 'Yes.'

Coroner: 'And the scullery window looks right down the yard and is at right angles to that?'

Anderson: 'Yes.'

The coroner asked whether they had heard anything other than the reports. 'Nothing more,' said Anderson. 'Miss Earle got up first and went to the back door. I followed. She opened the door and looked out, but could see nothing except a man who had just jumped from one wall to another.'

Coroner: 'Did you see him? What was he doing when you saw him?'

Anderson: 'He was lying almost full length upon the trelliswork on top of the higher of the two walls. Then he dropped down into the garden of Cambridge House, and we saw nothing more of him.'

Coroner: 'How were you able to see at all?'

Anderson: 'It was just light enough to see, but I think there was a moon ... not very much moon, but it was enough to see a man. We could hear a noise, too, – the crackling of the bushes and trelliswork. Miss Earle moved forward as though to go down the stairs. I called her back, and told her not to go down. She came in and closed the door, and went into the back room, which overlooks the end of the garden.'

Coroner: 'What is that used for?'

Anderson: 'It is now used as a sitting room; it was a bedroom when my father was there. We opened the window and looked out into the garden. We could see nothing in the garden, but we saw a few people in Rosenau Road, who had evidently been attracted by the shots. The only thing I saw was the reflection of a light in one of the back windows opposite the room in which we were, and I saw the shadow of a woman pulling down the blind. We then went back to supper, thinking some householder had surprised a burglar and had fired two shots to frighten him off, and that it was the burglar whom we had seen escaping. About a quarter of an hour after that Police Sergeant Buckley knocked at the door and Miss Earle admitted him.'

Mr Troutbeck questioned Anderson closely regarding his father. The young man said that it had begun to dawn upon him when Inspector Geake took him to Battersea Police Station that they supposed the dying man whom he had seen to be his father. Despite his father's visiting card having been found in the pocket of the deceased, Anderson was convinced that the dead man was not his father.

'Why,' asked the coroner, 'did you assume the card was found in the pocket of the dead man and not on the ground nearby?'

'That occurred to me also,' answered Anderson.

'Why,' Mr Troutbeck persisted, 'did it occur to you that the dead man might be your father, and not the man who was running away?'

'That is what occurred to me in the first place.'

The coroner: 'Will you tell us why it occurred to you in the first place it might be your father?'

Anderson: 'Because when Inspector Geake was taking me to the station his manner was such as to suggest I knew something of the affair, and he had found somewhere a business card belonging to my father.'

Coroner: 'These circumstances made you think in the first place it might be your father running away?'

Anderson: 'And, also, I was convinced that the man I had seen was not my father.'

Coroner: 'What convinced you of that?'

Anderson: 'Because he seemed to be wearing a moustache, and he (my father) was the last person I expected to see there. I saw the dying man before any suspicion of having anything to do with the matter occurred to me at all. All these notions came to me as I was being taken to the police station. I mentioned to my sister and Mr Badcock my suspicion that it was my father running away. I did not think it worthwhile. It was hardly a suspicion, but the whole thing was such a puzzle to me that all sorts of suspicions came crowding upon me, and that was one.'

Coroner: 'Have you got any explanation for the suspicion there was a moustache?'

Anderson: 'Yes. There was a black mark on the side of the face. I only got sort of general impression.'

The coroner, changing the direction of his questioning, switched to more personal matters.

Coroner: 'You know now there were certain relations between your father and Miss Earle. Did you ever know that your father was a very jealous man?

Anderson: 'No, sir, decidedly.'

Coroner: 'Did you know much about his affairs?'

Anderson: 'I knew a little. He was always reticent about his business affairs, but I know a good deal of his private affairs, but he seldom confided in anyone.'

Coroner: 'In trouble or worry he would never confide with a view to seeking sympathy?'

Anderson: 'He always kept it to himself.'

Coroner: 'Your father had said he might have come on this particular evening [16 July]. Would you have been surprised if he had come?'

Anderson: 'No, I should not have been surprised if he had been there when I arrived.'

Coroner: 'You did not know of your father's relations and intimacy with Miss Earle, otherwise you probably would not have gone there?'

Anderson: 'No.'

Coroner: 'Did you know whether your father was on similar terms of intimacy with any other person?'

Anderson: 'I am perfectly certain he was not.'

Coroner: 'You would have been perfectly certain he had no such relations with Miss Earle?'

Anderson: 'Yes, but I am also perfectly certain there were no others.'

Coroner: 'Had your father any personal enemy?'

Anderson: 'No, I could not conceive such a thing.'

A juror: 'Were any of your father's friends, members of the profession, in the habit of visiting Miss Earle?'

Anderson: 'I do not know of any.'

Inspector Badcock then made a final appearance confirming that since the last adjournment he had made full inquiries in connection with the case, and that he had no further evidence to put before the court. A great number of letters had been found at Miss Earle's flat, but, apart from those from Atherstone, none from men, other than on affairs of business. His subsequent inquiries had satisfactorily established the movements on the night of the murder of every person named.

Coroner: 'As regards Miss Earle's statement, you have had an opportunity of seeing whether it can be corroborated?'

Badcock: 'I have thoroughly tested it, and I have found her truthful in every particular.'

Coroner: 'Can you say the same about the sons?'

Badcock: 'Yes. They have all appeared to be anxious to help me.'

The coroner said that the police had followed up every possible clue and had endeavoured to get all information.

'It is quite clear,' he told the jury, 'that this case is as mysterious as it was during the first hour it was known to the police. Therefore, you are compelled to return an open verdict.'

They at once returned a verdict of 'Wilful murder by some person or persons unknown'.

The coroner thanked Inspector Badcock and his staff for the zeal they had displayed in dealing with the case.

Mr Humphreys applied that letters, etc. found in Miss Earle's flat might be returned to her. The coroner said that he could make no order, but would leave the matter in the hands of the police.

Thus was the Battersea Flat Murder relegated to the long list of London's unsolved murder mysteries.

And there, one hundred and five years ago, the matter ended.

10

Untidy Codicil

Well-guarded police files closed and stacked inconveniently away, inquest papers determinedly buried in remote cupboards of coroner's records; the murder of Thomas Weldon Atherstone presents a discouragingly unsatisfactory case. There was, and still is, even with access to every available scrivened inch of official paper, no solution to it. Not the faintest hint of what, if anything, was going on.

Unquestionably, the Battersea Flat Murder, as its contemporaries knew it, proffers what Sherlock Holmes would have designated quite a three-pipe problem. Overshadowed as it was by the Crippen affair, with its topsy-turvy corona of cellar burial, transatlantic drama and Marconi's new-fangled wireless, the Clifton Gardens mystery nevertheless commanded a countrywide fascinated attention.

The newspapers, surrounded by clouds of unknowing, set out to crystallise interrogatively the many-faceted enigma presented by the mansions' backyard shooting.

They asked,

Had the dead man reason to believe that someone might come to the back of the mansion premises?
If so, for what purpose?

Was Atherstone anticipating an attack on himself, his son, or Miss Earle?

Who was there with whom he had at any time quarrelled who might cherish sufficient ill-will to take his life, or bribe an agent to do so?

Who anticipated a possible meeting with Atherstone, and a possible attack by him?

What was the reason for the meeting, and the motive for the attack?

There were no answers.

In her *Riddles of Crime*, published in 1928, Isobel May Thorn, otherwise Elizabeth Villiers, an early writer of crime books, retails that the first idea afloat was that Atherstone's assailant was a lover of Miss Earle's, and that Atherstone, awash with green-eyed jealousy, had set to battle for her. Villiers claims to have met Atherstone and his wife and noted that the actor was an angry jealous man and their baby 'a forlorn mite, with bickering parents'. However, any idea that Atherstone's rival existed, other than in his tortured imaginings, had to be jettisoned when it became evident that Miss Earle had entertained no other lover and had remained absolutely loyal to the deluded Atherstone.

Nevertheless, Miss Villiers writes, 'It cannot be doubted that Atherston [*sic*] had gone to the flat that night thinking he would find some man with the lady, otherwise he would not have armed himself with that 'life-preserver'. Certainly, the presence of a home-made life-preserver in his pocket would seem indicative of the fact that when setting forth on his Battersea-raking expedition Atherstone had prepared himself for the possibility of a violent encounter of one sort or another.

Hargrave Lee Adam, in *Murder by Persons Unknown* (1931), thought it unlikely that the life-preserver was the sole weapon that Atherstone had taken with him. 'If it had been,' says Adam, 'it would hardly have been found in such an inaccessible place as his back pocket. It would have been in his hand or up his sleeve, which is the usual place for concealment of such a weapon.'

As Jan Bondeson has pointed out, H. L. Adam, an old-time, well-established crime writer, had good police contacts and would have been likely to have picked up the hint if the detectives had uncovered anything to Atherstone's detriment. Incidentally, it is Adam who claims, on what evidential grounds he omits to tell us, that 'there were plenty of witnesses as to Atherstone's eccentricities. Like Prince, who slew poor Terriss, he was regarded as a "mad actor". He was a familiar figure at certain refreshment haunts in the neighbourhood of the Strand.'

I have, in my pretty extensive researches, discovered no evidence whatsoever of Atherstone's being regarded as a mad actor; *au contraire*, he was admired, respected and personally liked in the provincial theatre circles where his dye was mainly cast. As to his familiarity 'at certain refreshment haunts in the neighbourhood of the Strand', they were the normal pubs and bars at which he would take a social tipple with theatrical agents from thereabouts from whom he was seeking work. And there is absolutely no hint of his having been a heavy drinker. Again, *au contraire*.

Edgar Jepson, contributing 'The Battersea Flat Mystery' to *Famous Crimes, Mysteries and Romances: The Great Stories of Real Life*, a part work edited by Max Pemberton in the thirties (reprinted as *Famous Crimes of Recent Times*), could see no reason why a rival of Atherstone's in the affection of Miss Earle should, instead of approaching in normal fashion by the main door and main stairs of the mansions, have gone to her flat by that bizarre route – climbing over walls and crossing back gardens – which exposed him quite unnecessarily to arrest as a suspect burglar. The man, avers Jepson, carried a revolver, and he adds 'at that time the habit of carrying revolvers was widespread among young criminals'.

In those Elysian days it was possible freely – which is to say without the legal let, hindrance and requirement of certification or documentation of any kind – to purchase, possess, and carry firearms. It was the social unrest before the First World War that intensified the pressure for gun control, and finally resulted in the creation of a licensing system for rifles and handguns after the war. Gun control gradually expanded in the 1930s, relaxed during the Second World War, and was then reinforced with full vigour.

Revolvers had begun to achieve mass popularity in 1851. Technologies advanced at speed, and by the 1890s revolver design had gone just about as far as it could. These guns got better and became cheaper. With the ongoing lowering of price, concern grew regarding the availability to criminals of cheap German revolvers.

In 1883, a pair of armed burglars in the London suburbs set off a round of press hysteria about armed criminals. The press notwithstanding, crime with firearms was rare, and in 1895 strong pistol controls were rejected by two to one in Parliament.

As the nineteenth century closed, buyers of any type of gun faced no background check, no need for police permission, and no registration.

Back in 1899, rector's daughter Miss Bertha de Spaen Haggerston Peterson, having purchased a six-chamber Colt revolver, for £2 7s 6d, and 109 bullets at the Junior Army and Navy Stores, slew John Whibley in her father's parish schoolroom, immediately after Sunday morning service on 5 February 1899. She had taken it into her decidedly disordered head that poor, innocent Mr Whibley, the village bootmaker and her fellow Sunday school teacher, had sexually assaulted a little girl named May Vane, who attended his Sunday school classes, and that he was corrupting village children. She claimed that God had told her to kill him.

Charged with murder, she appeared before the magistrates at Cranbrook. Wearing a large fawn hat bedecked with black feathers, and a fur cloak, she was perfectly, unaffectedly calm as she gazed smilingly through her pince-nez round the court at the horrified villagers, 'recognising this one and that with the assured condescension of a Lady Bountiful'. She was committed for trial at Maidstone Assizes, where the defence of insanity was not only supported by practically every prosecution witness, but her family history disclosed irrefutable proof of hereditary madness. She had been practising with her revolver in the woods. On 5 February she told her friends that she had wrongly accused Whibley, a married man, and invited him to meet her in the schoolroom for a reconciliation. He willingly went there. She showed him a picture she had bought entitled 'The Good Shepherd', and told him to look well at it. As he did so, she pulled out the revolver, placed it close to his ear, pulled the trigger and shot him dead. Found guilty but insane, she was sentenced to be detained during Her Majesty's pleasure. That meant Broadmoor, where she spent the rest of her life.

Perhaps in reaction to this, in 1903 Parliament passed the Pistols Act, which forbade sales to minors and felons and mandated a gun licence – from the GPO, for a fee.

H. L. Adam discusses the burglary theory for Atherstone's murder, arguing that it requires only a moment's consideration to realise its improbability. He points out that to begin with 9.30 on a summer's evening is much too early for armed robbers to be about their nefarious business. Moreover, the Battersea homes in question, those in the main of authors, artists and actors, were scarcely of the prosperity calibre that would attract the cupidity of the better class of professional cracksman, for they would be unlikely to contain any possessions of worthwhile value. He in fact believes that the killing was no murder, but that the revolver had been transported to the scene by Atherstone, who somehow contrived accidentally, in the course of a savage hand-to-hand struggle with a petty thief, to turn it upon himself.

Bernard Taylor, author of the account 'The Battersea Flat Mystery: The Murder of Weldon Atherstone' in *Perfect Murder*, a product of the joint authorship of Bernard Taylor and Stephen Knight (1987), confesses that he initially suspected Thomas Frederick Anderson and Elizabeth Earle as lovers and killers. He came round, however, to the view that only the burglary theory can be accepted.

Taking into account the circumstance that none of Miss Earle's friends – or Miss Earle herself for that matter – could suggest the name of any rival who might threaten Atherstone's amatory status, that the woman who waited upon Miss Earle at the flat had never seen a rival or any trace of one, and that there is moreover no evidence at all for the existence of any such Atherstonian enemy, Edgar Jepson, in his 'The Battersea Flat Mystery' in *Famous Crimes of Recent Times* concludes that there could be very little doubt that the murderer was a burglar, 'But,' says Jepson, 'doubt has been thrown on the theory that the footprints in the garden leading towards No. 17 were the same as the undoubted footprints of the man who fled away from it.'

Likewise, Elizabeth Villiers opines that the only sensible solution of the mystery is that Atherstone was shot by a chance-encountered burglar.

And that was the original official police notion. After a confident start in the belief that they were looking for a gun-toting burglar, the Battersea police underwent a radical change of mind. As Sir Melville Macnaghten, Assistant Commissioner (Crime), explains in his book of reminiscences *Days of My Years* (1914), 'About a month before [Atherstone's murder] police had received information that a gang of German burglars was at work on the south side of the river. They carried firearms, and if attacked, would not hesitate to shoot. It was suggested in some quarters that Anderson might have met his death at their hands.'

Comments Macnaghten: 'The theory was preposterous. Burglars don't start business at 9.30 on a summer's night, nor do they crack cribs which contain nothing.'

Equally dismissive was Arthur Lambton in his *Echoes of Causes Célèbres* (1931): 'An unsatisfactory case if there ever was one. The theory of burglary may be ruled out. One does not burgle an empty flat.'

There have been many putative explanations and conclusions advanced to play with. Some have found it irresistibly tempting to subscribe to the idea that the man who was murdered and the man who fired the dispatching shots were known to each other and had moreover been well aware of the likelihood of their meeting on the hallowed ground at Battersea.

Jonathan Goodman in his *Acts of Murder* (1986) comes up with the distinctly distasteful and not very persuasive suggestion that this may have been, could have been, a case of patricide. Might Thomas Weldon's son, Thomas Frederick, and Elizabeth Earle, Thomas Weldon's discarded mistress, have fallen in love? Stranger things have happened.

Thomas junior, his younger brother, William Gordon, their two sisters and their mother, to whom they were reportedly devoted, had all been cruelly deserted by Thomas Weldon. They may, hazards Goodman, have felt that 'the ultimate revenge would be sweet, or they may simply have chosen to rid themselves of Atherston [*sic*] rather than face the prospect of having him live with them, sponging on them, until he died a natural death.'

Goodman puts the rhetorical question: 'Did the brothers, with Elizabeth Earle, conspirators in a murder plot, perhaps come together at some secluded rendezvous, the three of them there to congratulate one another on a job well done and to drink a toast: "Good riddance to Thomas Weldon Atherston [*sic*] – a rotten parent, an unsuccessful actor, a lover who became expendable?"'

'I wish,' says Goodman, 'I could make up my mind whether I hope that they all lived happily ever after.'

What did in fact happen to them is only semi-revealed in short takes. Miss Earle moved from Clifton Gardens soon afterwards, retiring determinedly into the shadows whence she does not re-emerge. One might guess that she made the antipodean journey.

Thomas Frederick affords us a deathbed glimpse. We are aware that he left London soon after the murder, joining the Merchant Navy and becoming a seaman. By 1911 he was in New Zealand, and in the November of that year he joined the Federated Seamen's Union of New Zealand (FSU). He crewed on the *Squall* and other coastal steamers, took part in the 1913 waterfront strike, and served aboard the Union Steam Ship Company's Pacific Islands steamer *Navua*. He settled down in Auckland, where, on 30 October 1915, he married Mabel Eleanor Douglas. They raised a family of four, three daughters and a son. He became active in the Auckland branch of the FSU. Lanky, bespectacled and balding, he was popularly known as 'Long Tom'. After decades of trade union activism, not without some considerable degree of success, he died at his Takapuna home on 22 September 1964, admitting the wholesale theft over several decades of union funds, to the tune of some £8,000.

All that we know of the afterlife of William Gordon Anderson is that he attested to four years' service in the United Kingdom in the Territorial Army – Private No. 1292, C Company, 9th London Regiment – on 30 March 1911, and that he served in the First World War from 4 November 1914, surviving and being awarded the Victory, British and 14 Star medals.

One might do worse than give ear – and serious consideration – to the following throw-away lines from H. L. Adam:

There is another kind of petty sneak-thief who will fit the case very well. He is a paltry larcenist, who is always on the lookout for a door left open or a window unfastened, so that he may slip in and carry away anything portable, no matter of how little value it may happen to be. He may have been 'investigating' the backs of the flats generally, looking for open doors or unfastened windows, creeping from garden to garden, silently slipping over walls – a five-foot wall is not difficult to negotiate – closely peering at the backs of the houses, until he suddenly simply 'butted into' Atherstone.

As regards Atherstone's red diary, which he had kept since April 1910, it did indeed prove to be a most extraordinary document. Macnaghten observed that it exhibited a number of queer entries – 'Much of what he wrote was unintelligible, some of it indecipherable.'

A little penny memorandum book – a penny for your thoughts, or, rather, suspicions, for its entries were all jealous constructs, making it abundantly plain not only that Atherstone was deeply in love with Bessie Earle, but also that he positively haunted the vicinity of her flat in anguished expectation of coming face to face with another man, a rival for her hand and heart!

The names of four men were inscribed therein, underlined, as it were, with suspicion. 'It was obviously necessary that the police should find out who these individuals were, and what they had been doing on the Saturday night,' writes Macnaghten. 'After patient inquiries, which lasted over many weeks, all four men were cleared up; one, I think, was in America, a second in Canada, and the remaining two had not been in London for some time, so that, if any hostile feeling had been entertained against them, it was of no recent date.'

There were also in the little red book a great many entries listed under the heading 'B', which stood for Bessie, and a great many more standing contrapuntally under the heading 'A.W.', which stood for Atherstone himself.

Its pages exhaled the green-tainted breath of morbid jealousy.

Adam wrote, 'No doubt existed that the jealousy-tortured actor was crazy – jealousy itself is a form of mental distemper – and his premeditated attack upon an unknown rival was of a highly theatrical, melodramatic character.' All very well, but we do not know that Atherstone initiated the attack. It could well have been that *he* was attacked by the intruder.

On the other hand, one reporter wrote that several actors who had appeared with Atherstone told him that he appeared to be an unusually jealous man and ready to fly into a temper directly the least thing upset him.

Morbid jealousy, the Othello syndrome as the psychiatrists dub it – for Shakespeare's character may be said to epitomise the psychopathology of morbid jealousy – is a matter for serious concern. Generally speaking, the delusions of jealousy are usually based on the subject's false belief as regards the supposed infidelity of his spouse or sexual partner. Invariably, most dubious, not to say highly improbable, 'evidence' is proffered in support of shaky allegations. This is predominantly, although not exclusively, a male symptom, most frequently encountered in men who are heavy drinkers. Serious danger lurks, for violent and homicidal consequences may ensue. Around 5 per cent of cases end in homicidal acts. Particularly susceptible to the development of this syndrome are those who harbour suspicious or obsessional paranoid personalities. Equally, though, the onset of the delusion may frequently be sudden or explosive. Most commonly it manifests as part of another psychiatric disorder – such as schizophrenia, alcohol abuse or a depressive illness. The format of the psychodrama is typically along these lines. It begins with the subject accusing his partner of infidelity, citing some trivial evidence or some concatenation of improbable circumstance accumulated over a substantial swathe of time. This may then escalate into a prolonged, relentless interrogation, finally disintegrating into an undignified, offensive scouring of underwear or bedlinen in search of tell-tale seminal stainings.

So what, finally, is one to believe? What strikes as the likeliest upshot of the entire bizarre affair? To have once more resource to Holmesian sagacity, 'When you have eliminated the impossible, whatever remains, *however improbable*, must be the truth.'

I feel sure that, however impossible or improbable it may seem, the lengthy arm of coincidence was flexing itself that long-ago July night in the Battersea back garden. I am convinced that Atherstone encountered there an itinerant housebreaker, who, unlike most of his kind, had armed himself with a revolver before setting forth on his burglarious expedition. The slippered Atherstone, crouching in the sheltering darkness of the ground-floor flat, ears and every other sense alert, had caught the sound, faint and stealthy, of alien movement out beyond the half-open scullery door. Heart pounding, senses tight as the skin of a well-tuned drum, his whole being alight and alert, he had crept softly out into the menacing night, intent upon the destruction of the rival whom he had always suspected and feared. The intruder, as startled and fired up as his unknown threatener, unhesitatingly closed with him. Fierce battle ensued. The robber saw the prospect of his escape to freedom diminish as Atherstone's stranglehold upon him tightened. Desperate and afraid, he drew his gun and fired twice, blasting shots at lethally close range into his struggling opponent's head and face. Then took to fear-winged heels ...

Gathering his disciples around his deathbed, the old hermit told them, 'I've lived through some terrible things, my sons, and half of them never happened.' But thinking can make it so, make those things come tragically true, as in the sad, cautionary case of Thomas Weldon Anderson.

Appendix

Lionel Gadsden was eighty-six and still acting when he broadcast these memories. They are recorded in John M. East's *'Neath the Mask: The Story of the East Family* (George Allen & Unwin Ltd, 1967).

One of my dressing-room companions at the Lyric Opera House was an actor called Weldon Atherstone. He was very highly strung and temperamental. I saw him burst into tears when Jack East said, 'There's nothing for you in the cast next week, Weldon!'

I shall never forget going up to see Jack East at his office in Maiden Lane. It must have been early in 1910, and Weldon Atherstone was walking up and down in a distraught condition. Jack East came out of his inner sanctum, and Atherstone fell on his knees and screamed something like, 'She's been unfaithful to me, and after all these years! Laughing at me behind my back. Help me, Mr East, help me!'

Jack East gave him a sovereign, and that was the last I ever saw of Weldon Atherstone. A few weeks later he was murdered in Battersea.

As far as I can recollect his mistress lived on the second floor of Mansions in Prince of Wales Road. The ground floor was vacant. On that night Atherstone Junior was upstairs with his father's lady friend.

Meanwhile, Weldon Atherstone himself had broken into the empty flat below, changed into carpet slippers, and disguised himself with a false moustache. The police found an iron cosh in one of his overcoat pockets afterwards. As to his intentions, well nobody ever found out. He must have been disturbed by the murderer just after arrival. There was a struggle, he was shot twice through the face, and his assailant escaped by the way he had come – over the garden wall into Rosenau Road, never to be heard of again!

I assume the murderer knew that Weldon Atherstone was going to Battersea, or alternatively, followed him there from Atherstone's digs at King's Cross. The woman upstairs was a dramatic coach, and my own theory has always been that the murderer was a student actor who came between her and Weldon Atherstone.

When the police brought his son down from the flat above, he could not identify the corpse. The face was so mutilated, you see. When it came to the inquest they brought in the usual verdict – wilful murder by persons unknown.

It is interesting to discover that according to the scale of pay as reported applying to the stock company of the Lyric Opera House, Hammersmith, *c.* 1892, leads and heavy leads received a maximum of £6 per week.

Acknowledgements

I am most grateful to Stewart Evans for his assistance and many acts of kindness during the writing of this book.

Without the help so willingly offered by my friend Nicholas Connell my task would have been immeasurably more difficult. I am deeply indebted to him.

Another stalwart is Stephanie Bilton, who, however complex and complicated my need for assistance, most especially in the matter of tracking down obscure illustrations and the pursuit of abstruse genealogical research, has never failed me. My warmest thanks and gratitude to her.

Ever ready with rapid rescues and the clarification of obstinate problems has been Dr Jan Bondeson, for whose valued friendship and advice I am truly thankful.

As ever, I have relied upon much sound advice from my wife, Molly Whittington-Egan, herself an exceedingly capable author, with the same Battersea memories as myself; Albert Mansions, just round the corner from the murder flat, having been for more than twenty years our home beside the park.

Richard Whittington-Egan

Select Bibliography

Adam, H. L., *The Police Encyclopaedia* (Waverley Book Company, 1920), Vol. V, p. 23; Vol. VI, pp. 82–89

Adam, H. L., *Murder By Persons Unknown* (W. Collins Sons, 1931)

Armstrong, Anthony, 'The Battersea Flat Mystery', in *Great Unsolved Crimes* (Hutchinson, 1935)

De Loriol, Peter, *Murder and Crime: London* (The History Press, 2010)

Goodman, Jonathan, *Acts of Murder* (Harrap, 1986)

Jepson, Edgar, in *Famous Crimes of Recent Times* (George Newnes, N.D.) and in *Great Stories of Real Life* (George Newnes, N.D.)

Lambton, Arthur, *Echoes of Causes Célèbres* (Hurst & Blackett, 1931)

Macnaghten, Sir Melville, *Days of My Years* (Edward Arnold, 1914)

Oates, Jonathan, *Unsolved Murders in Victorian and Edwardian London* (Wharncliffe Books, 2007)

Taylor, Bernard & Knight, Stephen, *Perfect Murder* (Grafton Books, 1987)

Villiers, Elizabeth, *Riddles of Crime* (T. Werner Laurie, 1928)

List of Illustrations

13. The silent witness. This stone image, carved by the owner/builder above the front door of his house in Rosenau Road, 'saw' the running murderer pass by. The head was retrieved by the author when the premises was being demolished.
14. Cambridge House School and the binomial mansions, as seen from Rosenau Road.
15. Drawing showing details of the back area of binomial mansions.
16. The lay of the land and properties viewed from the front of Prince of Wales Road.
17. Ground plan of the empty ground-floor flat at the binomial mansions.
18. Edward Noice.
19. Emma Lewis.
20. Police Sergeant William Buckley.
21. Divisional Detective Inspector Edward Badcock.
22. Dr Felix Charles Kempster.
23. Dr Ludwig B. Freyberger.
24. Miss Earle hiding her face in the witness box.
25. Miss Earle in the witness box, her veil lifted.
26. Elizabeth Earle – her altered aspect after her ordeal.
27. Miss Earle in her stage days.
28. Miss Earle as she was in the beginning.
29. Official police photograph. Thomas Weldon Atherstone; his last curtain.
30. The final close-up.

Index